COPING WITH STRESS
IN CARING

Roy D. Bailey

MA (Hons psychol), DACP, ABPsS, MAPS
Principal Clinical Psychologist and
Head of Psychology Department
Manor House Hospital, Aylesbury

FOREWORD BY

June Bailey

RN, EdD, FAAN
Professor and Associate Dean
University of California

Blackwell Scientific Publications
OXFORD LONDON EDINBURGH
BOSTON PALO ALTO MELBOURNE

© 1985 by
Blackwell Scientific Publications
Editorial offices:
Osney Mead, Oxford OX2 0EL
8 John Street, London,
    WC1N 2ES
23 Ainslie Place, Edinburgh,
    EH3 6AJ
52 Beacon Street, Boston
    Massachusetts 02108, USA
667 Lytton Avenue, Palo Alto
    California 94301, USA
107 Barry Street, Carlton
    Victoria 3053, Australia

First published 1985
Reprinted 1986

Set by Colset (Pte) Ltd.
Printed and bound
by Billing & Sons Ltd,
Worcester.

DISTRIBUTORS

USA
    Year Book Medical Publishers
    35 East Wacker Drive
    Chicago, Illinois 60601

Canada
    The C.V. Mosby Company
    5240 Finch Avenue East,
    Scarborough, Ontario

Australia
    Blackwell Scientific
        Publications (Australia)
        Pty Ltd
    107 Barry Street
    Carlton, Victoria 3053

British Library
Cataloguing in Publication Data

Bailey, Roy D.
    Coping with stress in caring.
    1. Medical personnel—
    Diseases and hygiene
    2. Stress (Psychology)
    I. Title
    610.69'01'9   R690

    ISBN 0 – 632 – 01271 – 4

CONTENTS

FOREWORD

The aims of this book are to increase awareness and understanding among health care providers relative to the 'casualties of caring' , and to present practical ways for health professionals and organizations to manage stress more effectively. Numerous books address the major concepts and theories of stress, but few books provide the caregivers with tools and techniques to modify the ever increasing demands and stressors which touch the lives of each of them — nurses, doctors, therapists, social workers, educators, and other members of the health care team.

One of the themes of the book addresses the hazards and untoward outcomes which are inherent in the job-related work of health professionals. It is interesting to note that the health care profession has been identified as a stressful occupation, and that those who care and minister to others — the patients — are at risk with respect to their own well-being and productivity. This finding is not surprising when one recognizes that patients are sicker, more frightened, more subject to intrusive procedures, suffer more, and are often more demanding and difficult.

Another major theme of the book might be described as a road map. The map seeks to direct the 'caring' traveler to pursue certain pathways, to follow signposts, to pay attention to danger signals, and to use prescribed tools and techniques in order to avoid the pitfalls of a potential 'rocky road' which lies ahead of them in their daily activities.

A third theme presents an urgent plea for health care systems and providers to initiate and evaluate a Health Professional Consultation Service (HPCS) which is both preventive and restorative in nature. Not only is a loud and clear call for action made, but perhaps more importantly, the Health Professional Consultation Service is clearly outlined. Overall purposes, functions, criteria, benefits, and the economics of the service have been described; an HPCS model has been designed; organizational guidelines have been developed; and the importance of an evaluation of the program has been addressed.

Throughout these major themes, the author has intricately woven his own experiences as a therapist and researcher. The reader is presented with protocols to which he or she can relate, which gives real meaning to the complex, multidimensional phenomena of stress and coping.

It would appear that the author of this book has provided a challenge to the healing profession to test and adapt an effective way to manage and modify their own stress. In addition, organizations are admonished to provide support services to those caregivers who often care so much for others that there is little left in time and energy to care for themselves.

Coping with Stress in Caring is, indeed, a book whose time has come. In essence, it symbolizes what humanizing the health care environment and what 'caring for the caregivers' are all about.

June T. Bailey
Professor and Associate Dean
School of Nursing
University of California,
San Francisco

PREFACE

The caring and helping professions' many roles have one thing in common. They all strive to help their client and patient groups cope with different kinds of stress. Equally important but largely neglected is also the need for those who care and help others to find ways of coping effectively with their own kinds and levels of experienced stress. A myth has grown up around the helping professions that they are immune from the same sorts of stress-related problems as their patients and clients. The author calls this the myth of the healthy helper.

In this book the myth of the healthy helper is challenged and evidence presented which suggests another view altogether. This view claims that there are many in the helping professions who experience unpleasant and many forms of stress. This may influence their own health and the quality of service provided to those in their care. An attempt is made to show that many diverse groups of professionals may be experiencing difficulties in coping with the care which they provide.

Professional groups such as doctors, nurses, remedial therapists, and social workers, concerned with the well-being of their patients and clients seem to experience stress-related problems. These may range from being mildly discomforting to the more seriously alarming; such as 'caregiver burn-out': a complex stress state peculiar to individuals which can paralyse their functioning as helping professionals.

In an effort to ameliorate some of these difficulties, this book also concerns itself with coping. My endeavour to present a perspective on coping should help health professionals to deal with disabling stress when it arises, and prevent it in the future. Part of this approach shows how the helping professions can identify and recognize stress in themselves and each other, how it comes about and the different types of coping that might be applied to deal with it effectively.

The chapters are organized so that they may profitably be read in chronological order.

Chapters 1 and 2 describe stress and burn-out in the helping professions. In Chapter 3, a conceptual-practical framework for understanding stress and coping is outlined. This chapter also considers different dimensions of coping: such as individual and collective coping and how regulating our emotions can reduce stress. It is argued that there are two main modes of functioning which the helping professions can adopt, and within which different types of coping take place; these are restorative functioning, and preventative functioning. Restorative functioning is seen as being those aspects of coping which are employed to reduce stress when it has occurred, as being experienced by the particular caregiver. Preventative functioning is presented as the coping actions adopted by the individual or groups to minimise those demands of their professions which they anticipate they will be unable to deal with from their present coping repertoire.

To support the general theme of caring for caregivers, Chapter 4 presents a series of practical coping procedures which can be learned by the helping professions. These procedures are based on work done with other client populations, and coping clinics held for helping professionals working in the health care services. Chapter 4 argues that a high priority should be given to prepare and support the helping professions in their efforts to cope with the demands of caring. A number of proposals are made here, including the development of coping tactics and strategies based on stress management training. Chapter 5 shows how breathing is central to stress and the way we cope with it. This chapter also describes how correct breathing can be encouraged and utilized as a 'bridge' to stress control. In Chapter 6 I argue that more attention should be given to researching the helping professions' coping effectiveness; how it influences their own professional functioning, and the quality of service provided to different client and patient groups. An important development here should be the provision of services to health professions. One way of doing this is to establish models of Health Professional Consultation Services; where more effective ways of coping with stress in caring can be applied, researched and evaluated.

It is hoped that practitioners of the coping procedures in this book will benefit from them in their private as well as their professional lives.

Roy D. Bailey

ACKNOWLEDGEMENTS

Many people helped to make this book possible. I am especially grateful to:

Margaret Clarke, the Director of Nursing Studies at the University of Hull, for her continued encouragement to complete the manuscript.

The Oxford Regional Health Authority, who provided financial support for the research and the Aylesbury Vale District Health Authority, who allocated generous study leave.

Hazel Allen, the Assistant Director of the King's Fund Centre, London, who kindly arranged a visiting lectureship in Mental Health and Community Studies at the University of California, San Francisco, where I had time to prepare the ideas for this book and continue my research into stress and coping in the health professions.

June Bailey, Professor of Nursing and Assistant Dean at the University of California, San Francisco, who provided excellent facilities at the School of Nursing there.

Ann Baldwin PhD, at Stanford University Hospital, who has encouraged me to examine other consultation services for nursing and relevant to other health professions.

I would also like to thank personally David Chiriboga, Professor of Psychology with the Ageing and Human Development Project in the School of Medicine, at the University of California, San Francisco. It is David I have to thank for making it possible to meet and discuss stress and coping with Richard Lazarus, Professor of Psychology at Berkeley Campus, the University of California.

It is with a very deep regard that I thank Richard Lazarus for the many salient points he shared with me unselfishly and for making my visit to Berkeley a most salutory experience.

I am indebted to Bernadette Bailey, Senior Postbasic Tutor, Stoke-Mandeville Hospital, for some of her insights on the difficulties facing the ICU nurses and their practice.

I am also grateful to the Administrator and Medical Social Workers at Santa Barbara Cottage Hospital, California, for sharing some of their views on stress and coping with me.

Thanks go to the Association of Scientific, Technical and Managerial Staffs (ASTMS) for permission to include the job-appraisal scale on pp. 159–60.

Thanks are also due to the National Development Team (NDT) for use of their report, 'Improving the Quality of Services for Mentally Handicapped People: a check-list of standards produced by the National Development Team for the Mentally Handicapped', printed for them by the Department of Health and Social Security (1980).

I would like to thank Hazel Taylor for her secretarial support and Diane Gulland, Librarian at the postgraduate centre at Stoke-Mandeville Hospital, for the substantial computer research work she did for me.

Last, but not least, thanks go to Phyllis Holbrook and Judith Wilson of Blackwell Scientific Publications for their creative and efficient editorial advice.

LIST OF ILLUSTRATIONS

CHAPTER ONE

STRESS AND
THE HELPING PROFESSIONS

Stress is now recognized as being a hazard for those employed in the helping and caring professions. At some time or another we can expect to experience emotional and physical problems arising out of the demands of caring for people. A government health warning should be imprinted on every health professional's mind: 'Caring Can Damage Your Health'. In this book for the caring and helping professions, I hope to show this can, and does, happen. I also want to present ways in which undesirable stress such as anxiety, anger, frustration and fatigue may be combatted, overcome and even avoided. First, though, let me make it clearer, the way I am using the much abused word, *stress*.

ORIENTATION TO STRESS AND COPING

Stress has many definitions. Here, I prefer to adopt a perspective on stress that has a practical usefulness for caregivers in the helping professions. The best one I have discovered to date can be spelt out quite clearly.

Stress is not necessarily a 'bad' thing, it may be 'good' and this is sometimes called *eustress* (Selye 1980), and signals coping is required. But stress is often associated with those uncomfortable and undesirable states or feelings people have about themselves. These may involve their emotions and their physical condition. Central to this view, are the opinions we appraise, hold and express as being 'stressful'. In other words, what is stressful can largely depend on the way we think about ourselves and our circumstances. Putting this into psychological terms,

1

stress occurs as a result of the 'cognitive appraisals' we make of excessive internal or external demands we regard are being made on us at any particular time (Bailey 1981; Claus & Bailey 1980; Lazarus 1966, 1976; Lazarus & Launier 1978). In summary then, stress emanates from:

1   the way we think about ourselves and our circumstances
2   the meaning we give to the demands we consider are being made on us
3   the value we put on the importance of caring for others

At this point, I should like to draw your attention to coping. Coping can be productively defined as 'an individual's attempt to manage (i.e., master, tolerate, reduce, minimise, etc.) internal and external environmental demands or conflicts which tax one's resources' (Lazarus & Launier 1978). Notice this view of coping. It does not assume that all coping is successful, but are *efforts* to *manage* one's internal or external environments and the relationship he or she has with it. Second, it is concerned with change and this means seeing coping as a process (Folkman 1983). And third, just as stress can derive from these three sources and the appraisal of excessive demands, so too coping is inevitably involved and influenced by them as well. You have probably noticed this already in your own experience.

It makes sense. Whether stress is experienced, however, is a complex matter. It requires close observation and evaluation of the relationship between the way individuals and groups of health care professionals view the demands made on them and the coping they employ to manage, overcome or avoid stress. What we can say is that where the demands of caring are appraised as excessive or threatening, stress is likely when adequate individual and collective coping resources are not available. The helping professionals in the health care field who find themselves in this predicament may become what I call 'the casualties of caring'.

THE CASUALTIES OF CARING

Who are the casualties of caring? The now burgeoning research and clinical literature in the helping professions shows that stress is becoming a major problem for many caregivers. Reports and publications are amassing which confirm the predominance of pronounced stress problems amongst nurses, doctors, remedial therapists, radiographers, medical social workers, teachers, and other professions with the responsibility of providing client care and treatment (Bailey 1981; Claus & Bailey 1980; Lavandero 1981; Marshall 1980; McCue 1982; Cherniss 1980; Edelwich & Brodsky 1980). Clearly, society's casualties of caring can also be those professional agents who are expected to provide care to diverse patient and client groupings. Health professionals such as nurses and doctors in particular evidence a wide range of stress problems typical of the general population. I would go further than this and claim that because nurses and doctors and allied health professionals are more exactingly exposed to human suffering, they are at *greater* risk than those for whom they care. This may sound ironic and incredible to the reader. Sadly, however, I think this is the case. The demands of caring for others as researchers have shown can be extremely stressful (Bailey 1981; Cherniss 1980; Colligan *et al.* 1977; Marshall 1980).

The uncompromising message from these investigations and reports can be spelt out loud and clear. The responsibility and accountability of providing care for patients and clients who are handicapped, ill or infirm are often excessively demanding both emotionally and physically. The caring health professional is apparently inexorably subjected to demands which lead to considerable stress. Since the caregiving health professionals such as nurses and doctors are particularly at risk, what are the most common stress-related problems they experience? And, whom do they affect?

PROFESSIONAL TRAINING

Stress problems are evident for many nurses and doctors early in their professional training. The training seems to set 'professional' demands which are appraised as 'stressful'. This can even occur in the early stages of their career training. Many nurses experience their sojourn into nurse training as one of stress and reality shock (Kramer 1974). For instance, nurses and doctors soon find out that the demands of caring are not always in line with those which they may have been led to expect by the media and vocational counsellors (Sobol 1979). This appraised 'mismatching', or poor fit, between expectations and reality is an early source of stress for the aspiring professional caregiver (Bailey 1983a; Kramer 1974).

Anxiety seems to be a commonly recorded form of stress reported by nurse students (Birch 1979). This is also likely to be a problem for medical students and allied health professionals in training because of the student demands made on their time, dedication and concentration on their studies. Their training at present does not sufficiently equip them to cope with their own stress. The stressful appraisals made by nursing and medical students early in their training are also often due to poor professional relationships and failed social support systems (Kaplan 1977), as well as a lack of available individual and collective coping resources (detailed in Chapter 3). Frustration, anger and depression may be experienced during the professional training period by nurses and medical students. This is probably particularly intensified when the student is allocated to care for specific patient or client groups such as chronically ill children, the handicapped, the geriatric, and the dying (Birx 1983; Hooper 1979; Oswin 1971, 1978; Whitfield 1979).

Many students, early in their career paths, soon discover that caregiving is often stressful. Senior nurse students may also experience a wide range of appraisals as stressful. Appraisals are those assessments individuals make in order to derive meaning from each situation. Senior nurse protocols from my own staff-support clinic records suggest that senior nurse students may even be more pressured than their junior colleagues (Bailey 1981) in that more seems to be expected of them. They should 'know better' and 'make fewer mistakes'. I would think that a similar situation exists for students of medicine and allied health professionals.

Senior Nurse Students

Senior nurse students are not spared the exacting demands of nursing. Third-year nurse student stress protocols, that I have recorded, confirm that levels of stress which are difficult to cope with are not simply the naïve complaint of the novice nurse.

Protocol 1

Helen, a bright third-year nurse student in general training, recalls:

'I think I feel most stress in situations that are out of my control, i.e., when people are dying, and whatever you do does not alleviate their suffering, or when you cannot get your professional colleagues to do what you think they ought to do, and when you cannot get supplies and hospital backing for your patients to help fulfil their needs. It's not very nice when you have an old lady admitted as an emergency and there is not a night-dress to be had in the corridor.

'Difference in status can be stressful. One week you can be on nights and in charge, trusted with the lives of patients; the next week you can be back in school with a pupil nurse status.

'Also, it can be stressful on the wards — one day in charge, the next day it's back to the sluice. Personally, I feel I can cope with this, but I have seen younger nurses who are just beginning to "find their feet", gain confidence and responsibility, who find this very confusing.'

Helen makes the point of saying she is a mature student: 'I am thirty-two years of age and may not feel the same sorts of stress, or experience the same situation as stressful, as an eighteen-year-old.'

Helen's report shows how personal circumstances such as age and 'experience' may help nurses to combat stress they may experience at work. But it does not discount the fact that she has had to draw on this experience to be able to meet the demands of nursing, something which — she persuasively points out — younger nurse students in training may not have.

The immense range of demands that can be made on nurses either by others, such as their colleagues, patients or simply the high standards set by themselves, are such that it may be impossible to list all of those circumstances which give rise to stress and overwhelm an individual nurse's capacity to cope (Bailey 1981, 1983a; Marshall 1980).

Protocol 2

Michelle, a single, energetic and enthusiastic nurse student expresses the continuous kaleidoscope of demands made on her, and her views on coping:

'Starting on a new ward causes a certain amount of stress, depending on rumours you have heard from colleagues concerning that particular ward. Although it is obviously best that the nurse begins a new allocation with an unbiased opinion, it is difficult when you have heard that Sister X is a "so-and-so".

'Learning to use new equipment can also be nerve-racking, e.g., the first time you see "an actual, real, live patient" attached to a cardiac monitor. Even so-called simple procedures, such as carrying out dressings and so on, can cause stress, and how one copes with these situations depends a lot on the staff you have around you at the time. Someone who accepts that you are frightened and are bound to ask seemingly ridiculous questions will probably help you cope better that someone who tells you "not to be silly and get on with it".

'Death on the wards can lead to stress, some deaths being more depressing than others. It is easier, for example, to accept the death of a ninety-year-old dying peacefully in her sleep than it is to see a twenty-eight-year-old with three young children obviously fighting against carcinomatosis. Again, the behaviour of other members of staff contributes greatly to how you cope.

'For example, a man was admitted to a ward where I worked and died terribly (I thought) of a brain tumour — the picture still remains in your mind of someone foaming at the mouth and convulsing. I coped badly with the situation at the time, but luckily the sister on the ward was very understanding, and had it not been for the fact that she took me into the office and allowed me to voice my feelings (my own father had, in fact, died two months previously) I think I would have given up nursing there and then.

'I think that most nurses have days when literally everything seems to go wrong: bedpans, bowls of water and thermometers jump out of their hands; they forget to give Mr. Bloggs his suppositories, nourishing food or whatever. At this point you tend to go off duty thinking "Oh God, I am useless, I'm going to give up." You dread facing another day, which will probably turn out much the same. At times like this it is essential to have a friend or group of friends with whom you can share these experiences, and more often than not you end up laughing at the fact that you tipped a locker over during the consultant's round, instead of feeling an absolute failure. It is in this way that you cope with your stressful moments, and help your colleagues during their difficult times.

'Personal life does play an important part in your work on the wards, and can affect how you cope under stress. Trouble with boyfriends, trouble at home, e.g., death or illness of a relative, seems to be on your mind. Although you try to put these factors out of the way while you're at work, you are, after all, only human and can't simply switch off your feelings just because you have put on a uniform.'

Notice how coping with these stressful situations can be exaggerated through lack of support from friends and ward staff. Conversely, social support may allow collective coping to take place and act as a 'buffer' between demands of nursing or provide a means for direct coping (House 1981). This nurse illustrates fairly well how anxiety may be ameliorated through sharing experiences with colleagues and a 'we're in this together' feeling; this forms a kind of collective coping resource.

'Personally, coming into block training always causes stress — or it may be better called *anxiety*. Block tests, examinations and results are, of course, nerve-racking, but I think that being in a group undergoing the same sort of anxiety helps.'

Michelle has listed many of the difficulties with which many nurse students have to cope.

It will be clear from the individual reports I have listed, that many of the demands of nursing do not affect every nurse in the same way, and neither does every nurse cope with them in the same way. This raises a fascinating but frustrating problem: How then, are nurses to cope with the diversity of demands that are made on them, which can be threatening to the extent that they interfere with their personal and professional functioning? This problem is considered again later, when we look at practical methods of coping with stress.

THE QUALIFIED HEALTH PROFESSIONAL

Is the stress experienced by students in the health caregiving professions just a passing phase to be tolerated somehow? A rites of passage to be endured until graduation day and professional recognition? Then, is it no longer a problem? Unfortunately, but perhaps more realistically, this is *not* so. Studies of qualified health professionals substantially support this sombre conclusion.

Nurses

Sisters, charge nurses and directors of nursing and nursing services can also experience stress at work (Allen 1980; Arndt & Laeger 1970a, 1970b; Redfern 1979). Providing high role-load demands, with conflicting expectations of role behaviour of these nurses, seems to be the base of their stressful experiences.

Also, while sisters attempting to implement 'total nursing care' philosophies may be a justifiable potent aid in patient recovery and rehabilitation (Allen 1980), the very closeness often inherent in the nurse-patient relationship may present demands to many qualified nurses which are appraised as significantly threatening (Bailey 1983a).

Another 'pressure' nurses are likely to feel here is the demands of caring for the elderly and the dying, and the responsibilities of developing services for the handicapped and elderly (Chiriboga 1983; Hooper 1979). For instance, the loss of a patient may be not only appraised as a failure of medicine or professional nursing care but taken very personally by the nurse. However, some nurses may not feel the anguish, anxiety, anger, or despair often associated with a patient's death and dying. The nurse may also appraise a circumstance, namely death and dying, as one of relief for the patient, a peaceful escape from pain (Hooper 1979; Whitfield 1979).

This does not, however, alter an obvious, unpalatable fact: Many nurses are 'made' miserable by the death of patients and deeply saddened by the despair raised in their minds at the plight of the dying (Glaser & Strauss 1965, 1968; Kübler-Ross 1973; Lamerton 1973, 1978; Murray Parkes 1970, 1980; Whitfield 1979). In these circumstances, stress is likely to be quite complex and individual, taking several possible forms; for instance, anxiety, depression, anger, and physical complaints such as headaches and general aches and pains (Bailey 1984a). Put in more melodramatic terms, providing care and the delivery of services in the helping professions can be 'dangerous' (Murray Parkes 1980). The warning that *Caring Can Damage Your Health* should be regarded now with serious and concerned respect. It has some substance to it. Also, I believe this is one of the major reasons why many groups of nurses in the qualified grades have as high sickness-and-absenteeism rates as those undergoing their professional training (Bailey 1984a).

SOURCES OF STRESS AND SATISFACTION

Although stress is highly individual, and often a variable phenomenon, there are also a number of sources of stress which seem common to many nurses, and types of nursing. Commonly shared sources of stress seem to emanate from at least six areas:

1 Workload
2 Patient care
3 Interpersonal relationships with colleagues (e.g., nurses-nurses, nurses-doctors)
4 Knowledge of nursing and nursing skills
5 Types of nursing
6 Bureaucratic — political constraints

Interestingly, most of these sources of stress can also be sources of satisfaction for many nurses (Claus & Bailey 1980; Bailey 1984a; Birx 1983; Steffen 1980). For instance, lower workload and improved staff ratios, patient recovery, colleague support organizations and backing, and working within desired types of nursing, all provide satisfiers for nurses (Claus & Bailey 1980). But, why should essentially the same sources or nursing demands give rise to stress and satisfaction? I can see no more attractive explanation consistent with the view of stress than that which claims stress or its absence originates in the way nurses and other health professionals construe or appraise the demands of caring and the meaning it has for them within their present coping repertoire (Bailey 1983a).

A workload, for instance, may be objectively the same for two nurses, and the number of patients allocated or patient demands the same. One nurse may appraise these demands as a challenge to her organizational ability and an opportunity to apply some of the professional skills learned during professional training. The other may regard it as a threatening situation — undermining her professional competence — become 'edgy' and 'panicky' and disorganized in any attempt to cope with the occupational demands being made at the time. Just to make the point about appraisal of demands more emphatic, we can see how the same two nurses on another occasion may reverse their positions: The first appraising workload demands as threatening, and the second seeing them as a challenge to her nursing abilities. So it should be clear that it is not demands and coping ability in themselves which give rise to stress but the view that is taken of them. More poetically, 'there is', as Shakespeare observes, 'nothing either good or bad but thinking makes it so' (*Hamlet*, II, ii). This view is compatible with the fact that many nurses regard the same demands of nursing as sources of stress and satisfaction. Indeed, it points very clearly to the underlying complex mechanisms which can account for these apparent differences and agreements over sources of stress and satisfaction for nurses-cognitive appraisal (Lazarus 1966, 1976, 1981).

It is worthwhile keeping this in mind when acknowledging that there are several types of nursing which are characterized as high stress areas for nurses. The main ones seem to be: intensive care unit (ICU) nursing, mental handicap nursing, rehabilitation nursing, and medical-surgical nursing.

INTENSIVE CARE UNIT NURSING

Working in the paediatric and adult intensive care units seems to be particularly associated with considerable stress for many nurses (Bailey 1981; Birx 1983; Gardam 1969; Hay & Oken 1972; Huckabay & Jagla 1979; Michaels 1971; Vreeland & Ellis 1969). Hay & Oken (1972) pen a summary of life in the ICU which many nurses can identify with and recall from their own experience:

'A stranger entering an ICU is at once bombarded with a massive array of sensory stimuli, some emotionally neutral but many highly charged. Initially, the greatest impact comes from the intricate machinery, with its flashing lights, buzzing and beeping monitors, gurgling suction pumps, and whooshing respirators. Simultaneously, one sees many people rushing around busily performing lifesaving tasks. The atmosphere is not unlike that of the tension-charged strategic war bunker. With time, habituation occurs, but the ever-continuing stimuli decrease the overload threshold and contribute to stress at times of crisis. As the newness and strangeness of the unit wears off, one increasingly becomes aware of a host of perceptions with specific stressful emotional significance. Desperately ill, sick and injured human beings are hooked up to that machinery. In addition to mechanical stimuli, one can discern moaning, crying, screaming and the last gasps of life. Sights of blood, vomitus and excreta, exposed genitalia, mutilated wasting bodies, and unconscious and helpless people assault the sensibilities. Unceasingly, the ICU nurse must face these affect-laden stimuli with all the distress and conflict that they engender. As part of her daily routine, the nurse must reassure and comfort the man who is dying of cancer; she must change the dressings of a decomposing gangrenous limb; she must calm the awakening disturbed "overdose" patient; she must bathe the genitalia of the helpless and comatose; she must wipe away the bloody stool of the gastrointestinal bleeder; she must comfort the anguished young wife who knows her husband is dying. It is hard to imagine any other situation that involves such intimacy with the frightening, repulsive and forbidden. Stimuli are present to mobilize literally every conflictual area at every psychological developmental level.

'But there is more: there is something uncanny about the picture the patients present. Many are neither alive nor dead. Most have "tubes in every orifice". Their sounds and actions (or inaction) are almost inhuman. Bodily areas and organs, ordinarily unseen, are openly exposed or deformed by bandages. All of this directly challenges the definition of being human, one's most fundamental sense of ego integrity, for nurse as well as patient. Though consciously the nurse quickly learns to accept this surrealism, she is unremittingly exposed to these multiple threats to the stability of her body boundaries, her sense of self and her feelings of humanity and reality.

'To all this is added a repetitive contact with death. And, if exposure to death is merely frequent, that to dying is constant. The ICU nurse thus quickly becomes adept at identifying the signs and symptoms that foretell a downhill trend for her patient.

This becomes an awesome addition to the burden of the nurse who has been caring for the patient and must continue to do so, knowing his outcome.'

The combination of diverse demands experienced by the nurse culminates in an inexorable workload. The workload is formidable — even in periods of relative calm. Many tasks, which elsewhere would be performed by nurses' aides, require special care in the ICU and become the lot of ICU nurses. Changing a bed in an ICU may require moving a desperately ill, comatose patient while watching EKG leads, respirator hoses, urinary and intravenous catheters, etc. Moreover, the nurse must maintain detailed records. Hay & Oken (1972) sum up the plight by observing that the ICU nurse has 'no place to hide'.

Amongst the further complications of ICU nursing are the breakdowns in communication between nurses and physicians (Birx 1983; Claus & Bailey 1980; Hay & Oken 1972; Huckabay & Jagla 1979; Steffen 1980). Confirming more systematically the vivid picture portrayed by Hay & Oken, stressful factors noted by Huckabay & Jagla (1979) showed four main areas of concern for the ICU nurse:

1 Patient care
2 Interpersonal communication
3 Environment
4 Knowledge base

These concur with some of the sources mentioned earlier. Ranking these for their stressfulness, Huckabay & Jagla (1979) endorse the view shared by nurse students that patient care and communication between colleagues and physicians can be major sources of stress for the ICU nurse. Of particular interest in this study though was how the notion of internal or external control might be related to factors regarded as stressful in the ICU. Briefly, internally orientated individuals believe that they have control over events in their environment. Conversely, externally focussed people tend to believe that events in their surroundings are not controlled by themselves, but largely determined by others — particularly those regarded as important and powerful (Rotter 1966; Lefcourt 1976). In nursing, these 'determiners' might be seen to be high-ranking nurses and physicians.

On patient care, Huckabay & Jagla (1979) have this to say about the ICU nurse and control:

'. . . the patient care category represents the ICU nurse with threatening situations that are controlled externally rather than internally and are therefore more difficult to direct and control. For instance, the death of a patient and the amount of physical work cannot be controlled by the nurse through either learning or experience and were, therefore, rated as more stressful [p. 24].'

Similarly, the problems of communication between nursing staff and physicians is interpreted by Huckabay & Jagla (1979) against internal–external control theory: 'The physicians and persons in the nursing office are seen as superiors who have dominance over the nurse. Situations involving them are externally controlled and therefore perceived as highly stressful.'

These systematic research accounts mirror much of Hay & Oken's original descriptive study of the ICU and nurse stress. Perhaps, because of the excessive, continuous and variable demands of the ICU, Michaels (1971) has gone so far as to ask if the nurse of the ICU is 'too much in need of support to give any?' However overstated this may appear nurses often have to make novel attempts to cope with the demands of the ICU environment. They may also do this in ways which are confusing to the public at large and easily misunderstood by those not associated closely with intensive care unit nursing.

Coping with the ICU

Support in coping with stress often comes from the nurses' own group. There is a general tacit agreement that 'we are in this together' (Kaplan et al. 1977). This form of collective coping has been called 'social support' (Caplan and Killilea 1976). Humour seems to be one of the main weapons that the ICU nurses share with each other as a means of giving each other social support. This could appear to the public as an anathema and abhorrently unrelated to the despairing plight of many patients and their relatives in the ICU. As Hay & Oken (1972) note:

'. . . it comes as a surprise to an outsider to observe routinely some of the nurses in the ICU joking and laughing. Even whistling and singing may be observed, phenomena which are inexplicable and unforgivable to distraught relatives. Some of this ebullience arises as a natural product of friendly behaviour of young people working together. But a major aspect is gross *denial as a defence* against their stressful situation [my italics, p. 14].

A liaison psychiatrist was proposed to help ameliorate some of the stress experienced by nurses working in the ICU. But this would do little to defuse the demands ICU nurses have to face unexpectedly and the emergencies encountered each day. Crisis is the norm, not the exception in the ICU. The formidable demands of the ICU are inevitably undertaken by nurses. This is the fact of ICU nursing. Few occupations can be characterized by such repetitive exposure to human suffering, dying and death. Nurses who have contact with death and the dying patient inevitably have to find ways of coping with the demands this places on them (Whitfield 1979).

The threat of losing life runs counter to the common perception that nurses 'save' lives (Menzies 1960; Nurse 1975). Nurses who attribute the loss of a patient as a personal or professional failure may be storing up trouble for themselves and in the care they provide to other patients. Denial then may sometimes be a justifiable defence to adopt when facing extremely threatening and unremitting demands in the ICU (Bailey 1983a; Lazarus 1983a, 1983b; Menzies 1960). Coping might also be effected by adopting a 'defence distancing' approach to patient care: back to diagnosis and bed numbers and away from total patient care. However, it does not need a clairvoyant to see this creating additional problems for the ICU nurse, and setting back the development of nursing theory and practice decades.

Compounding the problems already mentioned are the heavy workload schedules ICU nurses have to operate and the lack of professional gratification from unresponsive patients, unappreciative relatives and 'difficult' doctors. Little wonder that the self-esteem and confidence of the ICU nurse is often undermined (Claus & Bailey 1980; Bailey 1983a; Wellenkemp 1983).

To be sure, problems connected with the lack of social and professional support for the ICU are seen as adding to the burden of nursing, and the demands the nurse has to carry in the ICU (Hay & Oken 1972). These difficulties seemed to be intrinsic to 'the nature of the work'. Here, communication conflicts and breakdowns in professional understanding among physicians, relatives and hospital administration are not uncommon.

The conflicting demands placed on nurses in the ICU raises one of the telling paradoxes of total nursing care: It means 'being close' to patients whose lives are highly dependent on the ICU nurses, their colleagues and the use of sophisticated technological equipment. Paradoxically, it would appear that in the very focussing of the nurse-patient-colleague relationship, stress may be *inevitable* if nursing care is to be practised effectively (Bailey 1984a). Such a state of affairs leaves us wondering what additional means of coping nurses have in the ICU which might help *them* to alleviate their periods of experienced or anticipated stress. I make some suggestions on how this might be tackled in the chapters on controlling and understanding stress, coping, breathing, and stress management training.

MENTAL HANDICAP NURSING

Another area of nursing associated with stress amongst nurses is mental handicap (Bailey 1982a, 1983a). Feelings of alienation amongst nursing staff working in hospitals for the mentally handicapped is common (Moores & Grant 1977). One of their main concerns was the lack of involvement in making decisions which has a direct bearing on the care provided for the mentally handicapped. With the mentally handicapped, nurses do *not*

often control care decisions or how nursing care might be practised.

Maureen Oswin (1971, 1978) has been a major catalyst for
change in the conditions under which children lived in long-stay
mental handicap hospitals. Most of this change has influenced
the institutional policies of mental handicap hospitals; some of
which no longer admit children for long-stay hospitalization. But,
little seems to have been done to remedy her equally com-
passionate concern for nurses working in long-stay hospitals.
She observes that these nurses are often placed in a similar position to unsupported parents, having to find ways of fending for
themselves and attempting to cope on their own without complaint. Such pressing demands and unsupported mental handicap nursing rapidly results in many 'intolerable' demanding
situations which nurses have to face. The main problems were
attributed to:

1   Unfulfilled work expectations
2   Lack of social support as a means of collective coping

Oswin (1978) also suggests that many nurses employed in long-
stay hospitals suffer the same sort of depression that affects
unsupported parents. She goes so far as to conclude that:

'In effect, they were suffering from what I term *professional
depression*. This was especially obvious amongst qualified staff,
and it poses the question of how fair it is to train nurses and then
leave them unsupported in stressful situations which inevitably
will destroy their professional enthusiasm [p. 82].'

Many nurses in the long-stay hospitals for the mentally
handicapped reported being disappointed in their aspirations
about their work. Many felt frustrated because they were unable
to change the structure and policies of an institution which they
thought obstructed professional development and even pro-
moted poor patterns of child care. Nurses in mental handicap
long-stay hospitals had little opportunity to influence and control
changes they regarded as important for an improvement in child-
care practices and job-satisfaction. These are points which echo

some of the stress-related problems raised by the Moores & Grant (1977) study of nursing staff employed in hospitals for the mentally handicapped.

From these studies, and my own counselling clinic records of staff working in institutional care facilities for the mentally handicapped, we can conclude they experience different forms of stress which are generated through lack of adequate support to cope with the demands of their job. We can go further than this and say there is inadequate support for nurses in this particular area of nursing. This is likely to leave many nurses feeling helpless and generates lowered morale, motivation and depression (Seligman 1975).

We cannot avoid the controversial conclusion that one potential consequence of these sad circumstances may also be a deterioration in standards of patient care. Paradoxically, it would seem mental handicap hospital nursing may make occupational demands which handicap the nurse, as well as making institutional life unacceptable for many of the patients.

Fortunately, since Oswin's work (1971, 1978) government policy has begun to emphasize the need to develop comprehensive community service facilities for the mentally handicapped. The National Development Team in mental handicap in the UK has helped to draw up guidelines for how this might be done and how life might be reconceptualized and restructured for the mentally handicapped living in hospital and the community (NDT Third Report 1979–1981). Yet, policy and reports exhorting change have a peculiar penchant for meeting staunch resistance. We can expect rapid individual change towards community-based services for the mentally handicapped to be painful and slow. In the meantime, it has to be said that at present, although outdated facilities exist (Bailey 1981, 1982a) no substantial provision has been made for health professional staff support services or for mental handicap nursing counselling facilities compared to those now beginning to be developed for general nursing in the USA (Baldwin 1983).

Urgent attention should be given to the establishment of counselling clinics and staff-support groups for nurses working in mental handicap. Attention could also be focussed on those who nurse in hospitals for the mentally handicapped, and some of the community nurse training facilities now being pursued (Bailey 1981, 1982a, 1984c). It is timely, *and* overdue, to remember and act on Nurse's (1975) urgent invocation:

'Signs of stress and strain in those with whom we work need to be recognized, and once recognized, understanding support and help *must* be given [my emphasis, p. 12].'

Note how particular attention is given to identifying stress and developing coping procedures for overcoming stress.

REHABILITATION NURSING

Nursing patients who have suffered sudden vascular accidents, burns, malignancies, amputations, progressive degenerative disorders, and brain or spinal cord injuries is also a source of stressful experiences for nurses (Gunther 1977; Kübler-Ross 1973; Moos 1979; Stone *et al.* 1980; Marshall 1980). These injuries and conditions can be extremely threatening to the psychological and physical functioning of nursing staff.

In practical terms, working with highly distressed patients also increases the risk of nurses suffering from various emotional and physical complaints (Gunther 1977). From a psychoanalytic framework, Gunther suggests that this may arise from unresolved conflicts in the personalities of patients and nurses. This is unsubstantiated by any evidence and is an assumed interpretation of the causes of stress amongst nursing personnel employed in rehabilitation medicine.

In my own terms, the threatening and excessive *demands* on nursing staff in rehabilitation medicine can inevitably lead to considerable stress for many nurses. This phenomenon is one of 'the burdens of rehabilitation' (Gunther 1977); a burden which many nurses often have difficulty in coping with effectively and managing the stress involved (Marshall 1980).

MEDICAL-SURGICAL NURSING

Parkes (1980a, 1980b) has paid particular attention to nurse student stress associated with medical and surgical wards for male and female patients. Her results are quite detailed, but for our consideration it is worth noting that students showed:

1 higher levels of anxiety
2 depression
3 lower levels of work satisfaction

on medical wards compared with surgical wards. Parkes also found an important feature connected with the work environment in this study. Surgical wards seemed to have:

1 involved students more
2 better peer cohesion
3 staff support
4 autonomy
5 task clarity
6 more control rules over work behaviour by senior staff

The sixth finding seems at first sight to be a contradictory result (Parkes 1980a, 1980b). One explanation could be that the lower scores on these indices for the medical wards allowed the students to 'distance' and defend themselves more from patient contact (Barton 1977a, 1977b). If this is so it seems to support Menzies' (1960) classical comments that denial is a common form of defensive coping used by nurses.

On male and female wards, two differences were noted on social climate variables: Peer relationships and staff support were more friendly and supportive on male wards (Parkes 1980b). Viewing these issues against sexual attraction, Parkes suggests following a policy of mixed sex patient-nurse ward allocations wherever possible. This is one way in which stress may be ameliorated for nurse students. I concur with Menzies (1960) and Lazarus (1983a) that denial defence is a common way of coping. However, now more research is required on the efficacy of policy change in nursing practice, especially as it relates to stress amongst nurses. Yet there can now be little doubt that nurses, like their medical colleagues, in many ways are engaged in an increasingly demanding and stressful profession.

Doctors

Doctors are not immune to the demands associated with the medical profession. As Merrison (HMSO 1975) noted in the enquiry into regulating the medical profession 'nobody who had seen the detailed evidence presented to us would underestimate the nature and scale of the problem of the sick doctor'. Doctors display a considerable range of stress problems — some of them substantially serious. The range of problem areas can go from the mildly medically unfit to the generally unhappy and anxious doctor to the more serious impairments of human functioning. These include psychiatric problems, alcohol abuse, drug dependency, family discord, divorce, and suicide (Allibone *et al.* 1979, 1981; Bennet 1982; McCue 1980, 1982; Murray 1976, 1978, 1983; Sakinofsky 1980). A closer examination of the size of the stress problem amongst doctors can be better appreciated when we look at some of these areas in greater detail.

PSYCHIATRIC PROBLEMS, DRUGS AND SUICIDE

There is a high incidence of psychiatric difficulties in doctors, their marriages and narcotic abuse (Allibone *et al.* 1979, 1981; Crammer 1978; McCue 1982; Fine 1981). In the USA, one study reports a 20-year follow-up of 45 physicians who were originally described as 'psychologically sound'. On follow-up, they found that a large number continuously engaged in self-medicating with drugs or regularly abused alcohol (Vaillant *et al.* 1970, 1972). In the UK, the medical profession has also expressed its serious concern about drug dependency and alcoholism amongst doctors (Irvine 1982; HMSO 1975).

There is mounting evidence that self-prescribing is associated with a gradual increase in drug-dependency amongst doctors (Allibone *et al.* 1979, 1981). These measures can also be seen as maladaptive coping efforts by doctors to deal with the stressful appraisal they make about the demands of caring for patient populations, professional relations and family life. Clearly, some forms of coping can only lead to increased stress, and a complication of symptoms, leading to a breakdown in doctors' ability to carry out their professional responsibilities. Sometimes, the position may be so desperate that doctors burnout or take their own lives (Bailey 1983a; HMSO 1978; Murray 1978; Rose and Rosow 1973).

Perhaps the most worrying phenomenon amongst doctors is their alarmingly high rate of suicide compared with the general population (Blachly *et al.* 1968). Suicides amongst doctors in the UK, for example, is reported by the Registrar General and repeatedly shows that doctors are particularly prone to killing themselves. A 1978 report indicated the frequency of this appalling problem. Doctors in the UK are nearly 3.5 times more likely to commit suicide than those in the general population (HMSO 1978). Similarly, suicide is a pressing problem among physicians in the USA. One study found that whereas 11 out of 100,000 in the general population committed suicide, this number mushroomed to 36 per 100,000 amongst male physicians. A staggering statistic. The UK and USA studies lay to rest any myth of the doctor being impervious to stress and suggests they are particularly vulnerable to the demands of coping with caring. Being a doctor means being exposed to a high stress-risk occupation.

Suicide has been seen as an extreme form of stress. But, I believe that it can be more productively construed as an attempt at a *final coping solution* (Bailey 1983a) to end circumstances which are no longer bearable to the helping professional. If this view is correct, medicine and its relationship — health — to physicians and their marriages makes demands which they appraise as intolerable. As a consequence, they may make desperate and maladaptive bids at coping with the caring they are attempting to provide within health care systems. It would seem therefore that doctors make inadequate coping efforts which are severly maladaptive in their consequences, for example, engaging in extreme self-injurious behaviours such as excessive alcohol consumption, drug abuse and other coping alternatives which may result in self-inflicted fatality.

SMOKING AND ALCOHOL ABUSE

Smoking has significantly reduced amongst doctors (Registrar General 1978). But is this good news? It is clear, for instance, there has been no alleviation of other health problems such as those I have already mentioned. In addition, the medical professional is still particularly vulnerable to cirrhosis, suicide, poisonings, accidents, and alcohol addiction (Allibone *et al.* 1981; Bennet 1982; Lloyd 1982; Murray 1978).

Alcohol dependency has been estimated as being 2.7 times higher amongst doctors compared with control subjects in their own class group (Murray 1978). Added to this tragedy is a greater misfortune. Alcohol-dependent doctors may also:

1 show poor prognosis/response to treatment
2 refer late, when their dependency is well-established
3 deny their dependence on alcohol
4 self-prescribe
5 have colluding colleagues
6 have difficulty in recognizing the problem
7 be reluctant, even hostile, to treatment
8 sometimes commit suicide
9 have psychiatric problems
10 have family difficulties and divorce

Also I see little cheer in the reduction of smoking rates amongst doctors in Britain when we consider the increased pressing problems of alcohol dependency (*BMJ* 1979; Lloyd 1982; Murray 1976, 1978, 1983). Interestingly, Lee (1979) has gone so far as to suggest that cigarette smoking may have *helped* doctors only temporarily to cope with stress. Smoking can be seen as a form of palliative coping (Lazarus 1981). It provides temporary relief. Giving up smoking may assist in the promotion of general health, but residual tension may remain and may be dealt with in other damaging behaviours such as increased alcohol consumption and self-prescribing of tranquillizers (Bennet 1982; Lloyd 1982; Murray 1978, 1983).

THE SIZE OF THE PROBLEM

Research figures show that we may be touching only the 'tip of the iceberg' (Murray 1976). Recent reviews and discussions suggest a much bigger problem (Murray 1978, 1983; Irvine 1982). In the UK, for example, it is estimated there may now be as many as 3 000 practising alcoholic GPs; many others have similar problems and other softer signs of stress (Allibone *et al.* 1981). The calamitous connotations of these claims is not made any lighter when we consider that out of 51 doctors investigated by the General Medical Council (GMC) between September 1980 and August 1981, 19 were classified as drug addicts or alcoholics. Put another way more than a third suffered from some form of drug or alcohol dependence.

We can draw a number of reasonable conclusions from these studies of doctors. They are that doctors:

1   evidence a diverse range of serious stress problems
2   engage in coping efforts which are often maladaptive and undermine their health
3   demonstrate an incidence of stress problems in excess of the general population

NOT ASKING FOR HELP — THE DOCTOR'S DILEMMA

An obvious and logical question you may ask is 'Why doesn't the doctor ask for help?'. A dilemma of tragic proportions seems to characterize the professional healer we know as 'the doctor'. But, the doctors' dilemma is simple. They have difficulty in asking for help for *themselves* (HMSO 1975).

One consequence is that the peculiar demands of the medical

profession are likely to increase the need for help rather than reduce it. Additionally, doctors may be unaware of their stress problems. Often they are connected with occupational demands (Fine 1981). Another problem occurs when doctors suffer some form of stress which requires immediate attention. It may interfere with their own health, and the efficacy of their medical practice. Patients may receive an impaired standard of medical care from doctors with stress problems who attempt to cope with them in an ineffective, maladaptive way. Societal expectations epitomize the doctors' dilemma well. Doctors are supposed to be 'healthy, wealthy and wise'. They are simply not 'expected' to be ill. It is what the doctor and the patient believe the medical role to be that often maintains the difficulties doctors or physicians have in asking for help for themselves. One thing we can be certain of, is that becoming and being a doctor entails demands which professional training has not equipped him or her to cope with effectively. Provocative as it may be, doctors are unable to 'heal' themselves because they *are* doctors (Bailey 1983a; Fine 1981).

PHYSICIAN HEAL THYSELF

Attempts have been made to provide a support service for doctors suffering from stress at work in the UK (HMSO 1975). A committee, 'the three wise men' as they have become known, investigates complaints by, not about, doctors who may exhibit difficulties in their functioning such as excessive alcohol consumption and afterwards slipping standards of professional practice. This system, however, has tended to penalize, warn, reprimand, and chastise doctors rather than provide some service to rehabilitate them and some sort of coping support (HMSO 1975).

Some improvements may be indicated by changes in the approach to doctors suffering from stress. The GMC has begun to tackle this problem vigorously. But, until an explicit formal social support system is established, which has preventive as well as a rehabilitative perspective, we can expect stress-related physical and psychological problems to continue amongst doctors.

Perhaps the first stigma that should be removed is disapproving of those doctors who seek help for their problems. Clearly, there is much research waiting to be done in this area, research which requires the medical profession to open up itself to examination. Amongst priorities must surely be to enquire further into stress and coping of doctors. Near the top of this list should also be the setting up and evaluation of doctor support services to evaluate the collective coping capacity.

Nursing in the USA seems to have moved further along this road than the UK medical profession by setting up nurse consultation services (Baldwin 1983). Other professional groups such as physiotherapists, occupational therapists, radiographers, social workers, teachers, dentists, and allied paramedical services might find it in their interests to pursue similar paths to aid and sustain their workers' functions.

Ideally, rather than having the cost of the development of separate support services, integrated facilities for all health professions could be developed, and run along consultation-interdisciplinary lines (Bailey 1984b). However remote these desirable developments in the caring for caregivers may be at present, there seems little doubt that they would play a central role in ameliorating stress for those people employed in the health professions.

SUMMARY

Clearly the demands of caring in the helping professions appraised as stressful are a major concern. There are four main reasons for the state of affairs:

First, the stress experienced by nurses, doctors and allied health professionals may interfere with their own health.

Second, the demands of caring may be appraised as so threatening and stressful that forms of coping adopted may actually exacerbate and seriously compound the difficulties experienced and reported by the helping professions.

Third, the forms of stress and the coping pursued by the helping professional may lead to serious deficiencies in patient service delivery systems.

Fourth, but by no means the least, the type of stress and coping adopted may progressively impair professional functioning to the point of '*burn-out*' — a topic which has gained growing attention in recent years and which should be of utmost concern to the health professions.

CHAPTER TWO

THE BURNT-OUT HELPER

So much concern has been generated over stress in the helping professions that a phenomenon known as *burn-out* has recently made its way into the research on occupational stress and coping clinics for caregivers (Ansell 1981; Bailey 1982b; Freudenberger 1974, 1975; Maslach & Pines 1977; McConnell 1982).

WHAT IS BURN-OUT?

Caregiver or helper burn-out has been defined in various ways. One definition suggests it is 'to fail, wear out, or become exhausted by making excessive demands on energy, strength or resources' (Freudenberger 1974). Cary Cherniss (1980), a psychologist who has spent much of his time researching and evaluating staff burn-out in the human services, sees burn-out as a disease of overcommitment. Others propose a more specific view of burn-out: it is the 'loss of concern for whom one is working' (Maslach 1976). Later in 1980, Cherniss portrayed burn-out as the 'withdrawal from work in response to excessive stress or dissatisfaction'. Experience in running burn-out workshops and clinics for stressed caregivers presented a transactional-process view: burn-out is 'a progressive loss of idealism, energy and purpose, experienced by people in the helping professions as a result of their conditions of work' (Edelwich & Brodsky 1980). Recently Maslach defined burn-out as 'a syndrome of emotional exhaustion, involving the development of negative self-concept, negative job attitudes, and loss of concern and feelings for clients' (reported in McConnell 1982). This view of burn-out sees the problem as a *response* to excessive stress.

28

Despite the apparent confusion over whether burn-out is a stimulus, response or transactional process, there is some agreement that it is characterized by a pronounced stress state over time (Bailey 1982a, 1982b). This does not mean that all caregivers in the helping professions must inevitably experience burn-out. Neither does it mean that when burn-out is evident in helpers that they will be able to recognize it in themselves. Paraphrasing the poet Robert Burns, we might wish, 'Oh that we had the gift to see ourselves as others see us.'

Where burn-out is present in different individuals of the helping professions, it may take a wide variety of 'symptomatic expression'. We need, it would seem, to know more about these forms of expression and the way the individual helper engages in transactions with the demands of his or her occupation. We will then be in a better position to understand more about burn-out and how it may be ameliorated in the helping professions. First, however, let's make the character of burn-out more explicit.

BURN-OUT: A SYNDROME

Herbert Freudenberger, generally regarded as the 'founding father' of burn-out, discusses burn-out and skillfully sketches out how helper burn-out takes place connected with the demands of caring for others, and the symptomatic expression it takes:

'What are the signs that begin to manifest themselves in burn-out? For one, there is a feeling of exhaustion and fatigue; being unable to shake a cold, feeling physically run down; suffering from frequent headaches and gastrointestinal disturbances; this may be accompanied by loss of weight, sleeplessness, depression, and shortness of breath. In short, one becomes psychosomatically involved in one or more ailments. These are some of the physical signs of burn-out.

'There are also the behavioural and psychological signs of burn-out. For example, the person who used to be a talker, now remains silent. We notice that he used to contribute to staff meetings, but now he sits in a corner and says nothing. Why? He may have become resigned to a hopeless situation. He is fatigued, bored, resentful, disenchanted, discouraged, confused. He feels futile and fed up, and cannot talk about it.

'Other behavioural signs of burn-out we should consider are, for example, the quickness to anger and instantaneous irritation and frustration responses. The burn-out candidate finds it just too difficult to hold in feelings. He or she either is, or feels, so overburdened that the slightest occurrence can set him [or her] off . . . a word, a felt slight, a small disappointment, not to mention an outright tirade, criticism, or abuse [1975, p. 74].'

The burn-out syndrome seems to manifest itself about one year after the health professional has begun working in health care. Burn-out may take place in many different symptomatic forms but there are a number of physical, psychological and emotional features in common (Freudenberger 1974). These can be distilled down into physical signs and psychological-emotional problems.

Physical Signs

Feeling of exhaustion and fatigue
Unable to shake off lingering colds, bronchial complaints
Headaches
Gastrointestinal disturbances
Sleeplessness
Shortness of breath
Skin complaints
General aches and pains

Psychological/Emotional Signs

Touchy and irritable
Easily moved to tears
Apparently unprovoked outbursts of anger
Marked sadness
Screaming and shouting

Unwarranted suspicion and paranoia
Avoiding commitments to caring
Lethargic

BURN-OUT: A PROPOSED SYNTHESIS

Though no agreed approach is yet settled on burn-out as a syndrome, these preceding common features make it useful from a clinical point of view to spot those health professionals who are experiencing personal difficulties. Practically, we can relate and understand the burn-out features as a pronounced stress state which can be further identified by noticing and looking out for them in ourselves and in our colleagues in the helping professions.

Other guidelines which we can use to identify progressively increasing stress and features associated with burn-out can be enlisted for assessment. One way of doing this is to compare the individual or group of caregivers' burn-out features with their previous level of psychological and physical functioning. The questions we need to answer here are:

Is there a loss of psychological functioning compared with previous psychological health status?

Is there a loss of physical functioning compared with previous physical health status?

If there is either psychological or physical loss of health over a period of time, what form does it take? (E.g., persistent colds, headaches, crying, irritability, etc.)

If there is evidence of the features associated with burn-out as a pronounced stress condition, what coping efforts has the person enlisted to overcome, ameliorate or avoid circumstances which are connected with his or her present level of functioning? and are these helpful or counterproductive in dealing with stress or burnout?

Answers to these questions should 'be placed within the assumption that much of the stress those affected are experiencing has arisen out of the view they take of the demands of caring and their efforts to cope with these demands (Bailey 1983a, Lazarus 1966, 1981). But, who are affected and what are the typical kinds of things those in the helping professions say about themselves which will give us clues to the presence of or absence of stress burn-out?

HEALTH PROFESSIONALS TELL THEIR STORIES

Reports collated at my staff consultation clinics show a close correspondence with the general features of burn-out. They also demonstrate that:

1 stress occurs across different helping professions
2 there is often a loss of previous psychological and physical functioning
3 burn-out has a number of common stress characteristics
4 stress is also manifested in a way which is peculiar to each individual

They do not always illustrate what they have done to try and solve their problems. What is clear is that where coping solutions have been adopted, they often do not remedy their difficulties of stressful functioning in any substantial way. In some cases things can get worse, e.g., continuing to make greater efforts to attend work when they are exhausted (Bailey 1983a, 1983b).

Protocol 3

A health authority physiotherapist expressed her difficulties in a depressed voice and made these observations:

'The main problems seem to stem from staff turnover and the demands of the relationship building with new staff. I also have to cope with everybody's problems and rivalry for leadership and my attention and approval. At one point, I thought all of my staff and the hospital administration were against me. I got very tense and found myself extremely tired. I then found I had a

series of chest infections. I didn't take any time off work. Though
I wanted to just get a break, a few days to recuperate. But I never
took it because of my responsibilities. When I eventually did get a
holiday, I got another chest infection. During this whole period I
did often consider finding another job.'

Protocol 4

The head occupational therapist of a community hospital for the
mentally handicapped had this to say:

'It's an endless repetitive struggle. We find ourselves
wrapped up in a cycle of new staff and new patients — all
making demands that we have to cope with. Much of the time I
feel as if we are getting nowhere in our efforts to help each other
and the mentally handicapped.

'One of the effects which I experience is, I become
mechanical — just like a robot going through the motions of
helping and caring. Yet being mechanical is all I am able to hold
onto for dealing with my low periods. I seem to get more low
periods these days. I can see myself going through the motions of
helping and caring and running the department. I try to say and
do the "right" things. The quality of my work then becomes poor.
The personal cost to me in all of this is a kind of "inner
screaming". It's saying, "How much longer can you go on like
this?" Now I find myself adopting evasive tactics and "going for
the soft option". I don't really know where it is all leading to.'

Protocol 5

A manager from a community special care unit for the mentally
handicapped expressed the way demands are made on her and
her experience of stress in this way:

'There are times when an avalanche of problems arise
together. They all seem to bunch up and have to be dealt with
very quickly. You're thinking, "Which one will I try to solve
first?" But there are always so many interruptions that I soon get

"heated" and irritable. No sooner is one problem out of the way
— the next is demanding and pressing to be solved. I find I then
build up a great deal of tension inside myself. I get headaches,
and on occasion I shout when I shouldn't. I am finding it increasingly difficult to put a brave face on things. The trouble is, I
don't have someone to turn to with my problems and difficulties. I
have to face up to all the pressures in this kind of work. I get more
and more "worked up" so that I get more and more agitated.
Sometimes I just can't cope with it any more.'

Protocol 6

A qualified nurse allocated to a male medical ward on a shift
system for seven nights on and six nights off, gives her
impressions of what it is like for her:

'Working nights fatigues me. I get bad-tempered and
disorientated. My concentration gets limited because of the
unusual work periods. If you work for long periods without a
break after eight nights you have no energy left for caring. I don't
think a good job can be done when I'm like this — so fatigued. It's
especially difficult for anyone who is learning to be a nurse. I
have often thought of giving it all up. You get so worn out and
pissed-off.

'The nights off do help aid some recovery and replenishing
your body but then when you go back, it starts all over again.
You're back to "square one". All of the feelings of fatigue, irritability, disorientation come back. It seems like a cycle that keeps
repeating itself. I don't know if I can keep it up. I'll be glad when
it's all over and I am back on days again.'

Protocol 7

A consultant psychiatrist in the health service reflected how the
way the professional demands on him induced considerable
stress and eventually eroded his own health:

'I wasn't aware of it happening. But I noticed I didn't want to see patients any more. When I . . . . . when I did see them I didn't really feel like listening to their problems. I found I became . . . . . well, tense and angry. My colleagues drew my attention to this — especially when for no apparent reason I would go into unpredictable outbursts of rage and anger. Another thing . . . . . . I couldn't think straight. I suppose it might have been connected with feeling worn-out and my energy being spent . . . . . . I started coming into work later . . . . . . holding fewer clinics . . . . . . and closing them prematurely.

'At the moment, I am a bit scared of it all. The truth is I seem to be getting worse. Maybe I could come and see you again — I mean from time to time.'

Protocol 8

Damien, a respected senior nurse, painfully recalled his experience:

'You know I really didn't know what was happening to me. I found myself getting so angry over the least little thing, my friends, my family and all of my colleagues. The funny thing . . . . . . it's true, I tried hard not to get angry. You know, bottling all of it up and trying my best to keep calm. Maybe I should have asked for help. But I felt embarrassed and frightened to. After all nobody would expect a senior nurse to need help for his "nerves".

'But things just got worse. I began to have difficulties in concentrating, I even found myself forgetting the routine things in my job — like mislaying patient records. Maybe it sounds stupid now but I ploughed myself more and more into my job even though I kept hearing a little voice inside me saying, "Pack it in, you can't cope". It all came to a head when I applied for a promotion. This involved taking on even more responsibilities. Anyhow, at the interview I started to shake. I couldn't control myself, and I just burst into a flood of tears. It must have looked strange to see a grown man and a responsible nurse breaking down like that . . . . . . I had reached the end of the line — I knew it there and then.'

Protocol 9

A community social worker working with the mentally handicapped reported:

'My colleagues and patients depend on me too much. I used to
love that part of the work. But now I think they drag me down to
the point where I am exhausted. Sometimes it is my own fault. I
can't say "No" to anyone who asks me for help. When I have
tried I feel guilty at turning them down. So I take cases on and
increase my caseload.

'All these demands drain my physical strength. Emotionally, I
feel trapped inside myself. There seems no escape from it all. It's
like being caught up in a perpetual treadmill. Occasionally, the
tension is bad, I just don't want to work any more. The only thing
that seems to keep me going is a kind of mental shutdown. I go into
a kind of automatic action. You know sometimes I don't think
about what I am doing any more. I definitely don't think about
how important my work is any more. I suppose it's just working
with numbers. At least seeing it that way helps me — it's part of
shutting myself off from caring. That and the dulling I get from a
good stiff drink . . . . . . at least it keeps me going. It's occurred to
me just now as I'm going over this with you . . . . . . well, I wonder
if I . . . . . . have stopped caring?'

Protocol 10

Jenny, an experienced radiographer, honestly admitted:

'You know, I hate to admit it but I dread coming into work any
more. It's strange, but it all seemed to happen soon after I came
here. It was different at first. We all worked as a team. But
. . . . . . I don't know, as time went by, I began to get feelings of
resentment. I suppose I felt I was being asked to do too much. Or
maybe it was the intensity of the work and the seriousness of
some of the injuries some of the patients had. I remember putting
to the back of my mind how anguished I felt — especially when I
saw so many people in pain. I must have just blocked all of that

out — to the back of my mind — I suppose. Not long after that I began to get terribly angry with myself — you know for putting up with it. I often ended up with a blinding headache — maybe it was all of the tension. In the end — well the last five months — I seem to just go along with everything. I just do what I have to do and no more. Perhaps I need another holiday or a new job. Anyway, (the job) doesn't interest me. I've lost my enthusiasm for helping people. What a terrible thing to say — you must excuse me . . . . . .'

Protocol 11

Stephen, a recently qualified physiotherapist, noticed that:

'During the first few months of this appointment I had lots of innovative ideas. I wanted to show patients how to help themselves. I started educational classes for patients and their relatives. I also wanted to do research on all of this but I didn't get much support. I think it was my new ideas and energy that must have put my colleagues against me. I'm not sure about that. But I did think every opportunity I created for bringing physiotherapy to people was thwarted. It made me feel exasperated and miserable. When I started to "fit in", I suddenly found I lost a great deal of my energy to do things. I suppose you would know . . . . . . I was bored. Is that typical? I have even started smoking again. For the first time I am wondering whether or not to carry on in this job even though I have only been here 16 months. Do you think I am not really suitable to be a physiotherapist?'

Protocol 12

Virginia had been an experienced physiotherapist for six years. She revealed how she felt just before leaving the Health Service:

'There were many times when I wanted to give it (physiotherapy) all up. What surprised me most is I can remember thinking like this as early as my first year in my job. I know it may sound odd but it built up over the years. I began to miss patient appointments. And what frightened me a little was forgetting. I forgot important things like the patients' names and when I was supposed to give them treatment. Occasionally, I even forgot what type of treatment they had been receiving. I would then get anxious and confused. I tried to cope with the demands made on me by postponing work commitments. But I just got more disorganized and panicky. There was no one at that time I could turn to for help. At least I could have used the opportunity to talk to someone in private about these problems. I suppose my main problem is I can't say "No" to anyone who needs help. So I took on more and more work. I realize now I was making matters worse. Earlier this year, I had what seemed like a minor nervous breakdown. I couldn't concentrate. I was still forgetting things. All my chaotic efforts to put everything right didn't work. I noticed I had a nervous tic in my eyes. I kept blinking and I started crying for no apparent reason. I knew then, I needed help. The only thing I could do was to give up the job. So now you know why I am leaving . . . . . . perhaps I will apply for another post when I've had a proper rest.'

These case profiles tend to support the perspective on burn-out spelt out by Freudenberger (1974, 1975). You can see similarities of symptom formation which give clues of the possible presence of a pronounced stress state commonly regarded as burn-out. What is missing in burn-out though is a process model of understanding these cyclic forms of stress, the demands that preceded them, or are associated with them, the selective efficiency of coping and dealing with stress.

HELPER BURN-OUT: A PROGRESSIVE STRESS PROCESS

A process view of stress leading to burn-out has been suggested and supported (Bailey 1982b; Cherniss 1980; Edelwich & Brodsky 1980). It is the process by which a previously committed professional helper disengages from work as a result of the appraised and stressful transactions experienced in the job. A cursory glance at the case reports I have presented shows the disengagement aspect of burn-out quite clearly. They also hint at a cycle, or process, or psychological stages of progressive burn-out, taking place over time. Fortunately, the main stages have been carefully documented (Edelwich & Brodsky 1980). The psychology of burn-out as a progressive stress process seems to fall into four main stages:

1 Idealistic enthusiasm
2 Stagnation
3 Frustration
4 Apathy

It is within the beliefs, nature and appraisal of health professional demands that the process of burn-out takes place. Here is an overview of the development of burn-out progressing through the stages of idealistic enthusiasm, stagnation, frustration and apathy.

Stage One

Idealistic enthusiasm is the time of high energy, high hopes and high expectations. The job is life and life is the job of caring. During this stage, the caregiver tends to bring high energy, high principles and keen motivation to achieve the goals of the chosen profession. Accompanying these psychological features, there is often an urgent desire on behalf of the caregiver to employ professional training in his or her particular field of helping. There is often a marked energetic endeavour to employ helping skills and make an observable impact on the patient or client groups. It is when these laudable but usually unrealistic precepts, principles, priorities, and goals, about professional demands come into question that the zealous helper begins to move into the stagnation stage of burn-out. This often happens towards the end of approximately the first year of employment (Freudenberger 1974).

Stage Two

During the transition from idealistic enthusiasm to stagnation, the caregiver is thought to slow down and already energy levels begin to deplete. Motivation is decreased, and precepts, principles, caregiver priorities, and goals are no longer pursued with the previous vigour that characterized the stage of idealistic enthusiasm. At this period, the caregiver is likely to begin to experience disappointment in the expectations about the job. Those who have reported burn-out in the helping professions typically remark that stagnation is like 'coming to the end of the road', to be at a 'dead end', and they 'cannot see any light at the end of the tunnel'. When this is prevalent, the caregiver is no longer in love with helping. Personal needs are no longer seen as being satisfied entirely by the job. Interests outside of work may become more important such as friends, sport, leisure, one's own family, and home. As Kramer (1974) has said, 'the honeymoon is over'.

Stage Three

With the stage of frustration, a radical reality reappraisal begins to take place by the caregiver, lacing its ways through the earlier phases of burn-out (Bailey 1983a). As time passes, the caregiver is considered to experience frustration with the efforts to achieve the high helping goals of the profession. They are often thwarted, and unrealized. Frustration arises from two sources. First, the caregiver may be frustrated through not satisfying client or patient needs. Second, the caregiver often may become frustrated because of sacrificing his or her own needs in order to satisfy the needs of the patients. Where such processes are present, and prolonged, caregivers are likely to move into the fourth stage of burn-out.

Stage Four

Apathy may permeate every aspect of a caregiver's attempts to provide care to the patients. Alternatively, apathy may present in highly specialized areas of a helping profession (e.g., caring for the dying). But, the common feature underlying apathy is the same. The caregiver tends to see 'the job is a job is a job'. This could also be a sign of impoverished coping. Often typical signs of apathy are arriving late and leaving early for patient appointments. There is usually a general 'giving-up' air about the caregiver; being mechanical, keeping to safe and secure routines are evident. This may be connected with islands of remaining effort to cope with depleting professional helper energy. Apathy seems to be the last resort, the caregiver's final attempt to deal with the ravages of continuing frustration. Needless to say, the apathy stage of the burn-out process is often sheltered under the umbrella of complaints, bickering and general job dissatisfaction. What is left?

INTERVENTION

Intervention is noted as a later stage of trying to cope with burn-out (Edelwich & Brodsky 1980). Intervention requires some initiative on behalf of the affected individuals to do something, on their own or with the help of others, about changing their present circumstances and how they may feel. Interventions do occur by individual health professionals and may take several forms. These may include problem-solving, emotional-processing or regulation of the emotions and collective coping efforts such as utilizing available social support systems. In this light, however, intervention is better seen as an active process when health professionals such as nurses, doctors, remedial therapists, radiographers and medical social workers, individually or collectively, attempt to overcome or dispel some or all of the pronounced stress associated with burn-out. Different intervention options may be employed consciously or unconsciously.

Some typical examples from the literature and my own clinic records are:

1 Leaving the job
2 Delegating responsibility to others
3 Going on training courses and conferences
4 Joining a team of colleagues
5 Increasing recreation alternatives
6 Exercise (e.g., aerobics, jogging, swimming, dancing, cycling)
7 Meditation (e.g., yoga, TM)
8 Arranging study leave
9 Altering the job description (e.g., changing the demands made by the health care organization)
10 Visiting the health professional consultation clinic

They are *not* arranged in any order of priority, and more intervention options no doubt could be generated. I have merely listed the ones which I find most common, and which seem to crop up frequently in the literature (Bailey 1982a, 1982b; Cherniss 1980; Edelwich & Brodsky 1980). I would like to make two main observations about these forms of intervention to alleviate pronounced stress burn-out:

First, notice that some of the options involve taking on *more* demands, such as increasing recreation and exercise. In contradistinction, others involve off-loading demands at work. Leaving the job, going on a conference or study leave and delegating responsibilities come into this category.

The second is that these interventions may not be effective in reversing or alleviating stress or the features of burn-out. Some may, however, permit natural psychophysiological recovery process to take place (Bailey 1983b, 1984a; Schultz & Luthe 1969). This is one explanation of the health professional who comes back 'totally refreshed' after attending apparently demanding workshops and conferences.

Other options seem to be used as a 'discharge fix'. That is to say, like palliative coping, it allows mind and body regulation to take place without changing the demands that are being faced by the caregiver. Running, swimming, dancing, and cycling may all permit this to happen. The discharge fix may be used just as it is needed; for instance, after a 'heavy and hectic day' it is better than 'kicking the cat'. Or, it may be practised regularly to combat further depletion of psychological and body resources. Paradoxically, these interventions — at least jogging and swimming — may also become addictive in themselves (Bailey 1984c). This is what Glasser (1979) calls 'positive addiction'.

Exercise options such as aerobics may, therefore, have positive effects for some health professionals but not for others. Certainly, many joggers report a feeling of calm, well-being and even ecstacy. But, there is also the possibility that these interventions may lead only to slaves of swimming and jogging. In other words, these interventions may have only short-term benefits for health professionals. Currently, there is a re-evaluation of the worth of aerobics exercise in maintaining and promoting human health (Bailey 1984c).

Finally, options for intervention might also entail attempts at collective coping and seeking social support. For instance joining a team of colleagues or a sportsclub may also facilitate openings for overcoming substantial stress experienced by health professionals. These options seem to have considerable clinical appeal. Many remain to be researched critically for their efficiency in counteracting the stress problems we associate with the term burn-out (Bailey, Chiriboga & Larson 1983). Visiting a health professional consultancy service may also be an option. But these are not yet available in the UK generally (Bailey 1981, 1982a).

It should now be clear from this examination of burn-out in the helping professions that burn-out is perhaps not a satisfactory term to explain what is happening to people experiencing extreme forms of stress. We can, however, retain the term burn-out to mean a descriptive label which refers to 'pronounced stress states' peculiar to individual health professionals. In addition, we can justify the idea of burn-out as a general guideline to progressively impaired functioning of health providers over time and context. Other than this, we should consider that burn-out is part of the broader spectrum of human functioning associated with environmental demands, stress and coping (Bailey 1982b, 1983a). Consequently, if we are to learn more about burn-out and health professional functioning, we should make more creative and systematic efforts to understand stress and coping.

VIEWING BURN-OUT WITHIN A STRESS AND COPING FRAMEWORK

There are a number of important reasons why burn-out can be more fully formulated within a stress and coping framework. The main reasons are:

1 the stress profile of the burnt-out helper is often highly individual and variable

2 we need to know about the demands the helper has to face

3 what if anything they do to cope

4 whether their coping is effective or not in overcoming the demands and tolerating experienced or reported stress

5 it is not clear whether there is such a thing as a burn-out syndrome

6 a more fruitful, conceptual and practical view is to see the features of burn-out as individual stress and coping profiles related to human functioning (Bailey 1982b)

HEALTH PROFESSIONAL BURN-OUT AND PATIENTS

Stress and burn-out are likely to be a problem not only for care-givers but also for those for whom they care — patients and clients. Caregivers who are burnt-out in their patient-care functioning raise a number of important questions.

Is patient care adequate when the helping professionals involved in that care are burnt-out?

If it is not, what influence does caregiver burn-out have on patient rehabilitation, recovery and survival rates?

What relationships exist here for particular caregiver–patient populations such as those found in general medicine, nursing, remedial therapy, psychiatry and mental handicap?

Does the state of a caregiver's stress and burn-out facilitate, retard or have a negligible effect on patients and their physical and psychological capacity for dealing with illness and mobilizing healing processes?

Many of these questions remain to be answered and deserve urgent attention.

In the meantime, assessing burn-out symptoms should be more useful and clinically helpful to health professionals if we place it within a broader framework of stress and coping. Doing this we can also bring a focus on the way in which the individual may explore the appraisal of professional demands and the development of alternative coping strategies. It should also account for the fact that not every helping professional will show the same burn-out profile, or that there are some who seem to be 'immune' to most of the symptoms of burn-out.

Stress and coping are irrevocably connected with environmental demands. Those in the helping professions have daily commerce with demands which they have to cope with more or less effectively. So burn-out symptoms should be seen as just one part of a relationship schema of environmental demands, appraisal, stress, and coping (Bailey 1983a).

Finally, placing burn-out in this framework can make it both unchanging yet subject to change, since it is part of a dynamic system of human activity to regulate professional functioning. On this note, there is optimism for the professional helper, for it holds out hope, remedy and the development of effective coping with the problems of stress associated with so-called burn-out. The first step on this route is a better understanding of stress and coping.

CHAPTER THREE

UNDERSTANDING STRESS
AND COPING

So far we have become familiar with some kinds of the stress experienced and reported by nurses, doctors and other allied health professionals. But, stress is not something that happens in a vacuum. This is something which you probably regard as obvious. Yet, it is important to realize. For stress as it occurs in the health professionals is usually accompanied in different contexts over time by coping efforts to manage to overcome the sources of stress and return the individual to a stable level of homeostatic functioning. Successful coping should then enable the professional helpers to continue competently with the provision of care, and in such a way which does not place more excessive demands on them. This will also help to avoid spiralling into repeated stressful experiences and progressively more serious problems of human functioning such as burn-out. In understanding stress and coping we should want to know:

1   the environmental demands being made upon us at any one time

2   the kinds of appraisals we make of these demands (e.g., whether we see them as a threat, challenge, heavy losses, irrelevant, or enhancing)

3   the coping enlisted to manage to overcome or avoid the sources of stress we experience or anticipate arising out of the way we appraise the internal or external demands connected with professional helping

4   the short-term and longer-term outcomes of coping as it affects our behaviour, thinking, emotions, and physical health

5   the duration and efficacy of particular modes of coping

In a general way we can see that the health professional studies and reports reviewed all reflect aspects interpreted within these five guidelines. For example, many of the nurses cited diverse demands in the nursing environment which were stressful. Looking at health professional burn-out we saw how pronounced stress states like these can originate in the demands delineated by the various health professions.

Regarding coping we can infer from the studies amongst doctors that many of the coping options such as excessive alcohol consumption or self-prescribing and drug dependency may provide temporary relief from anxiety and other more serious stress problems. In the longer term, however, these coping actions do not provide sustained stability or relief. They may even increase stress and lead to more serious complications such as cirrhosis, heart disease and suicide. So there may be short-term gains in such coping as self-prescribing or excessive alcohol consumption with long-term losses to the helper's health. The intriguing but frightening aspects are that, many professional helpers:

1   are not conscious of the demands being made on them
2   depend on the appraisals they make of the demands
3   depend on the way in which they attempt to cope
4   depend on the outcomes of their coping

Making this more explicit provides an important start in understanding coping with stress in caring.

A MODEL FOR COPING WITH STRESS IN CARING

I have found that placing demands, appraisals, coping, and outcomes into a feedback flow-model (see Fig. 1) is a useful analogue for getting to know more consciously our own stress, coping and its relative effectiveness. It also allows us to organize what we know about ourselves as helpers in relation to the professional demands we regard as important or trivial and are being made on us at any given time. Also, the model can be applied to any set of internal or external demands and professional circum-

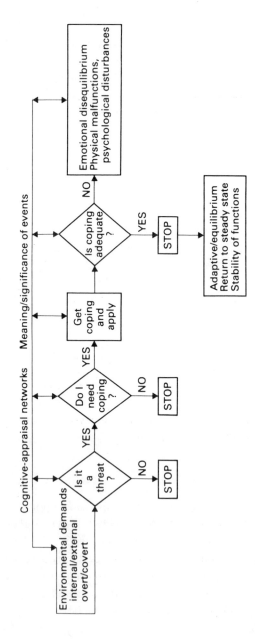

Fig. 1   Dynamic self-regulation flow-systems model for stress and coping.

stances. It is also possible to take into account whether these are overt or covert demands. A good example of overt demands is workload. This can be quantified for instance by the number of shifts worked. These demands are overt and can be made quite explicit. On the other hand covert demands are implicit. Covert demands often involve camouflaged communications, for instance the patient who expresses anger may really want to know if he is dying. Finally, it is possible to evaluate the influence that our coping has on ourselves, our surroundings, managing stress, and relieving us of stressful encounters.

Assumptions behind the Stress and Coping Model

The flow-system model procedures work like this: The individual appraises or processes demands from the environment and in doing so monitors the environment. Those demands which are irrelevant or neutral get no coping attention, or already have sufficient coping operating effectively so as not to proceed any further.

Thus, we reach the next point in the procedure. If coping is required, it is either consciously or unconsciously selected so we *get coping*. This may be in terms of restoring equilibrium and stability to the individual, or increasing malfunction or psychological and body systems. Notice also that it is possible to reappraise any aspect of demands of stress and coping and monitor the influence it has had on any part of the system. For instance, we can reappraise the demands being made on us, the significance they have and whether coping has changed our self-functioning in an adaptive or a maladaptive way. In this way the flow-model of stress and coping allows for both stability and change in professional functioning. The flow-model of stress and coping can also be seen as a dynamic system which has to account for psychobiological equilibrium, but because this is predominantly an active process I call it *dynamic self-regulation* (Bailey 1983b).

Practical Description

The model of stress and coping can be practically understood in this way. Supposing an external demand is appraised such as the nurse being confronted by an emergency admission from a road traffic accident. This unconsciously or consciously initiates coping by dynamic self-regulation. It is an attempt to alleviate the nurse's own, and the patient's, anxiety. If this is successful, the demands no longer are threatening to the nurse and the particular form of coping is terminated.

Another example might be a health professional who regards the covert demands on him or her of a dying patient as a potential loss requiring coping. Coping might alleviate that patient's pain, but not the inevitable outcome of death. The health professional in these circumstances may become angry, anxious or despairing. Coping then might also be simultaneously aimed at alleviating the personal anxiety, venting anger or 'letting go' of his or her attachment to the patient. This is palliative coping; it does nothing to change the source of stress, but is adapted and focussed on regulating the emotions of the health professional involved (Bailey 1983a, Bailey & Clarke, in preparation).

Moreover, other coping in similar circumstances may be maladaptive in the short-term and the longer-term as well. For instance, running away from the source of the stressful experience may set up a style of learning to avoid the responsibilities and demands of health care practice (Bailey 1984b). Longer-term problems are as we have seen often those associated with smoking, excessive alcohol consumption and drug dependency. So this flow-model clearly shows that:

1   not every demand need be stressful to the health care professional

2   it is possible to evaluate highly individual appraisals of professional demands

3   coping need not always be successful; that is, a reduction in experienced or anticipated stress is not guaranteed merely because they have tried to cope with the source of stress

4   a profile of what is demanding, how it is appraised, what coping is enlisted, and the outcomes this has on the professional helpers own functioning can be established

THE STRESS AND COPING PROFILE

Using this approach, we can draw up for ourselves, our colleagues (and indeed our patients) stress and coping profiles. These are likely to be useful in many ways. For instance, identifying those specific situations which are sources of stress and those in which we are coping well. We can also identify those sources of stress where we cope badly or only well in the short-term but have deleterious longer-term consequences. Most of all we shall have begun to focus on the meaning of demands on our own functioning; how it affects us, our client groups and professional colleague responsibilities. Profiles 1 to 12 demonstrate the role of measuring appraisal and coping efforts to manage or to prevent stress and maintain individual equilibrium.

Stress and Coping Profiles 1–12

Demands	Appraisals	Coping efforts	Outcomes
Profile 1: Marjorie			
Being repri-manded by Sister in front of patient.	Threat — loss of face. Felt anxious and embarrassed.	Asked to discuss the matter in private.	Went to nursing office to talk the matter over. Felt relieved and comfortable again.
Profile 2: Jane			
Dying patient.	Harm/loss of patient.	'Bottled-up' my feelings and put brave face on things.	Had a migraine, felt numb and miserable.

Demands	**Appraisals**	**Coping efforts**	**Outcomes**
Profile 3: David			
Dying patient.	Challenge to nursing skills.	Employed counselling techniques. Listened to patient's worries, stayed with him.	A patient died without apparent pain. I felt satisfied I had done all I could for him and was glad he died peacefully.
Profile 4: Karen			
Insufficient knowledge of treatment procedure.	Threat — felt flustered and inadequate.	Bumbled way through, and attempted to bluff colleagues.	Risk to patients and complaints from colleagues.
Profile 5: Linda			
Insufficient knowledge of treatment procedures.	Challenge to professional competence.	Conducted library research, and observed treatment procedure.	Felt more confident and relaxed.
Profile 6: Bob			
Being asked to work too many hours, and excessive patient responsibility.	Challenge to my endurance.	Tried high protein diet and jogging.	Exhausted. Reported to staff health centre. Ordered to rest.
Profile 7: Steve			
Poor results in examinations.	Irrelevant — just bad luck.	Not required. Did not pursue study path or learning resources facilities.	Failed state examinations. Felt angry.
Profile 8: Amanda			
Poor results in examinations.	Challenge — could do better.	Invested time in study plan and enlisted	Increased pass grades in school exams. Gained

Demands	Appraisals	Coping efforts	Outcomes
		resources at library and learning centre.	distinction in state final examinations.

Profile 9: Mary

Nurses', administrators', doctors' 'political' conflicts and disagreements about the way hospital is managed at Executive meetings.	Threat to the present routine. Do not want change.	'Shouted-down' any arguments against the established position.	Did not listen to my point of view. Changes instigated. Think of changing jobs. Upset and angry.

Profile 10: Zena

Interprofessional conflicts between nurses and doctors.	Challenge. Professional competence on trial.	Arranged professional liaison meetings and informal social meetings.	More open exchange of ideas and reduced conflicts.

Profile 11: Geoff

A colleague who is insulting and questioning skills competence.	Threat to own status — felt angry.	Enlisted the opinion of head nurse to mediate.	Anger was defused and the reasons examined, for colleague's attitude.

Profile 12: Sandra

Death of a patient.	Loss and anguish. Cloud of despondency drifted over me.	Went to staff support clinic, one visit each week for six weeks. Carried out autogenic regulation training.	Felt supported and let out suppressed feelings. Accepted the loss more readily.

Process and Practice

Stress and Coping Profiles 1–12 indicate the unfolding nature of stressful episodes for individuals, but can be appropriate for groups of health professionals as well. They also indicate that change is taking place. This may simply be in the movement from appraisal to coping to outcome and how it influences short- and long-term health. A profile can also show the changes which take place during and the outcome of coping efforts by health professionals. This often entails promoting altered appraisals, emotions and more effective coping behaviour. What is happening when this is going on? Each profile also suggests that stress and coping is a continuous dynamic process dealing with both change and stability of individuals and group functioning. As we can observe in the individual profiles, it is possible to identify what was going on at different stages of demand, stress appraisal and coping. A major objective of the health professions whose aim is to ameliorate stress and promote more effective coping in themselves and others is to take into account the process of stress and coping which affects them. As you can see from the profiles this is a complex matter. But it can be done with careful analysis using the flow-model (see Fig. 1) alongside stress and coping profiles. There is, however, a need for more information about the stress and coping processes which are relevant to human transactions with the environment (Lazarus 1983a). In time, these may become more easy to specify for groups of health care professionals. In the meantime, in clinical practice we can begin to record, store and use data which shows how individual and group stress and coping are relevant for professional caregivers. To be able to get a firmer grasp of stress and coping processes we can learn more about:

How individuals and groups process and act on the demands they believe are being made on them and are important for their practice as health professionals

What health providers actually do during stress and coping transactions with their environment

Where demands, stress and coping take place — the context of stress and coping transactions
Who is involved in the stress and coping episodes and what significance they have for health professionals engaged in stress and coping exchanges within caring contexts
When stressful episodes take place, their duration and consistency or change over time

Many complex questions are being raised about stress and coping and are the subject of a detailed programme of continuous research (Bailey 1984a; Lazarus 1983a). Clinicians and health care practitioners can help this effort by recording and examining the way in which they process environmental demands connected with health care, the way they act on them and the outcomes of their coping efforts to accommodate or bring about change and still maintain stable functioning. A valuable start can be made by establishing a library of stress and coping profiles for health professionals who need help, have sought help, and those who seem to cope effectively. Accounts should also be kept of systematic interventions to improve the health professional's sense of coping effectiveness or self-efficacy (Bandura 1977).

The Significance of the Model and Profiles

Combining stress and coping profiles with the flow-model we can see a number of important points which are validated conceptually and practically useful:

First, it can be observed how similar demands may be appraised in different ways.

Second, different coping efforts may be mobilized by the health professionals to move, alter, prevent, or overcome the sources of stress.

Third, the outcomes of coping may or may not alter the original source of stress appraised in the environmental demands.

Fourth, coping efforts may not change the demands being appraised but they might change the health professional's feelings such as anger, anxiety, irritability, and sadness. The change of feelings may be for better or worse. Consequently, coping is either adaptive or maladaptive. This is what is meant by effective and ineffective coping.

The stress and coping profiles therefore are interpretable against the flow-model in Figure 1. Additionally, the recording of the health professionals' stress and coping in profiles for specific and general demands associated with their profession aids us in a better understanding of stress, the initial reaction to it, what brings it on, how stress-producing demands are appraised, and how effectively it can be dealt with over time. This, as we can see, largely depends on the *meaning* given to the events in the environment and how they may be managed by each individual.

PROBLEM-SOLVING AND EMOTIONAL PROCESSING

The two main functions utilized during stress and coping are problem-solving and emotional processing (Folkman & Lazarus 1980; Lazarus 1966, 1976; Rachman 1980). Problem-solving skills acquired during the professional training of the health carers may be deployed as forms of coping. Emotional processing may also be used such as anxiety and anxiety-reduction training. There is no inherent assumption that one is preferable to the other, or set pattern as to which form of coping should be adopted. I would say this is also highly likely from the health professionals' point of view.

At present, patients' demands and caregiving priorities seem to emphasize problem-solving approaches to coping with the hope of effective outcomes, i.e., a return to stable functioning. This should permit the application of professional skills for the benefit of client groups.

When the health professionals require to overcome or express emotional problems, this need might be assisted through making available formal and informal social networks, such as staff support services (Bailey 1984c; Baldwin 1983; Kaplan

1977). A place should be made available in or near the professional setting where they can explore the meaning demands have on them, how they cope and the influence various coping efforts have consciously or unconsciously on their professional lives (Bailey 1982a). Additionally, counselling facilities (Bailey 1981; HMSO 1972) for preventing or reducing undesirable forms and levels of stress should be offered. These provisions should then ensure at least three perspectives:

1 *Prevention*: counselling services and stress-management facilities should be made known to health professionals, encouraging them to utilize them on a preventative basis

2 *Restoration*: counselling and stress-reduction facilities should also be made available for those in advanced stages of stress to restore equilibrium and stable functioning

3 *Staff support services*: facilities 1 and 2 (counselling/ stress-management/stress-reduction) should be presented early on in the professional training as part of the over-all staff support services available to those embarking in the health professions

DEFENCE MECHANISMS

Short-term

Defence mechanisms are ways of coping (Bailey 1983a; Bailey & Clarke in preparation; Lazarus 1983a). They need not necessarily be signs of psychopathology. Most of us use some form of defence mechanism every day, and, in many instances it is justifiable and healthy. For instance to deny the terrible significance of dying may be important for many nurses and health professionals working with the severely handicapped, the maimed and children with chronic diseases. They may find a positive value in passive denial.

Short-term denial to alleviate anxiety may help the nurse to carry on with nursing. Similarly, intellectualizing the approach to surgery may be of some coping efficacy to surgeons and

theatre nurses. Other defence mechanisms such as the employment of suppression, and the detachment, may make 'space' for
the health professional to mobilize more open forms of problem-
solving when emotional expression as means of coping with
stress is inappropriate. Being aware of this is probably one of the
most difficult things to develop. It should help to restudy the flow-
model and draw up profiles which reveal whether we are using
defence mechanisms and what form they take in our professional
process. Encounters with colleagues and patients and their
families, doing this can also show how effective defence
mechanism coping can help deal with the demands of caring and
the effects it has on health professionals and the services they
provide.

Long-term

In the short-term we have seen that there are temporary benefits
to be gained from defensive coping (Lazarus 1966). In the long-
term, however, relying solely on defensive coping efforts is likely
to raise adjustment problems for health professionals and
patients alike (Glaser & Strauss 1965, 1968; Lazarus 1983a;
Stone et al. 1980). To those concerned with stress and coping in
the health professions it is helpful to focus on where and when
defensive coping is used and what effect different kinds are
having on professional helpers and their services.

Does defensive coping help both the caregiver and the
patient? Is it only of benefit to the health professional and not the
patient? Is more complexity present? It may serve an adaptive
function for the health professional and the patient, but at other
times in relationship to the context of the service provided. How
do you make problems for health care experienced? Another
question which I find worthwhile pursuing with health professionals is: At what point does defensive coping become
counterproductive and stressful in itself? Those of us in the
health professions who may be concerned for colleagues as well
as ourselves need to answer these questions honestly. We can
start by researching and evaluating them against the flow-model

of stress and coping and drawing up stress and coping profiles of health professional functioning, and their relationship to patient care (Bailey 1983a). In the short-term defensive coping is likely to bring some benefits to health professionals. Putting problems 'to the backs of our minds' can help us to deal with current crises and job demands. Judged on the longer-term, however, defensive coping such as denial, and projection (e.g. blaming others) can lead to stored up stress. By storing up stress you then run the increased risk of burn-out and becoming one of the casualties of caring. I think the lesson to be learned is clear. Long-term defensive coping can take its toll on our mental, emotional and physical health.

WHAT DO STRESS AND COPING MEAN?

As yet, no definitive statement has been made on the meaning of stress and coping. Research continues in this area, and from the way stress and coping are presented here, there are a number of reasonable conclusions we can make:

First, stress and coping seems to be a dynamic set of processes.

Second, these processes are intimately connected with the meaning each individual gives to their cognitions in relationship to the demands in their environment and the coping they regard is available from individual and collective resources.

Third, the health professional does not necessarily have to go through the sequence of demands, appraisal, coping efforts, and outcomes. As the flow-model indicates, the individual or group can interject at any point (e.g., the health professional who wants to prepare for a particularly pressing set of demands, such as sitting state final examinations, can prevent undue stress by pursuing systematic courses of study and practise examination-taking techniques).

Fourth, coping efforts need not always be problem-solving based or emotion-focussed. Defence mechanisms may be employed as forms of coping.

Fifth, not all forms of coping lead to effective and desirable outcomes for those in the helping professions.

Sixth, it also makes it possible to check if sources of stress emanate not from health care demands but from other life areas such as the family (Bailey 1982b). However, adopting the approach to stress and coping I have outlined, we can clearly evaluate effective coping, i.e., those ways of coping which we find are especially 'good' at dealing with stress.

Finally, the flow-model of stress and coping highlights the importance of the meaning environmental events have for the individual, his or her welfare and stable functioning. These two, individual meaning and stable functioning, are in a sense the core antagonists in stress and coping.

These core antagonists give rise to the paradoxes of coping and caring (Bailey 1983a). In coping we are in a sense always attempting to maintain or make active efforts to return to equilibrium — the stable state. Conversely, we are developing human beings whose main task is coping with environmental *change* and in helping others, we also seem to be trying to make sense of ourselves and what we are about. This is imperceptible changing; yet we strive to maintain stability and equilibrium in the face of all changes in ourselves and our lives as private individuals and public health professionals.

I believe that it is within this framework of change, unfolding personal meaning and efforts — both conscious and unconscious — to maintain stable equilibrated systems that stress is created and where coping takes place. I also believe that it is within these very same parameters that interventions can be made to manage undesirable stress, and restore stable equilibrium where stress is already evident. The total system of coping with stress and demands is what I call *dynamic self-regulation*. For me this seems the fundamental purpose of any intervention: to regulate the relationships between the environment, the meaning an individual derives from demands in his life, his appraisal, how the demands are coped with, and to what effect.

INTERVENTIONS

Interventions with or by the health professionals for themselves and their patients should essentially be to facilitate dynamic self-regulation. This can be done in four ways:

1 altering the meaning of demands in the external or internal environment
2 acquiring professional or behavioural skills or erasing those skills which do not facilitate dynamic self-regulation
3 regulating emotions
4 collective coping (through the organization of social support systems)

Altering the Meaning of Demands

Suppose you were asked by a dying patient to tell him his prognosis. This demand may be appraised as stressful for the nurse, doctor or medical social worker. The coping which would follow from this appraisal might initiate denial of the patient's demand or lead you to ignore him or bottle-up your feelings of inadequacy. Altering the meaning such demands have for us, however, can also bring about different coping efforts.

Let us reconsider the same patient and request. This time you appraise the demand as meaning a *challenge* to your counselling skills. Coping this time is aimed at listening to the patient, reflecting back that you are with him and hear him and his plight. Surprisingly, you find that the patient says this is the first time anybody has found time to 'really listen' to him and it is a great comfort. So changing the meaning of demands can alter how environments are appraised, the coping employed and the outcome of coping. This has many ramifications for health professionals and clients in their care. It is impossible to exhaust the myriad of meanings which may be carried out during appraisals of health care demands and the way health professionals process them. This example, however, provides a snapshot of the type of interventions that can be made adopting interventions aimed at altering meaning of demands on the professional care provider.

Endorsing and Erasing Professional Skills

PROBLEM-SOLVING SKILLS

Developing problem-solving skills to cope with professional demands and stress is part of what nurses, doctors and other health professionals do during their training. An example is carrying out resuscitation procedures with patients who have gone into cardiac arrest. The skills involved enable the health professional to respond appropriately to the specific demands being made.

Skills in procedural competence need to be developed by health professionals until they become 'second nature' to them. When professional skills are honed to a high level of competence, they are not only learned but 'endorsed' onto the range of skills which are performed with ease and precision. When a health professional is said to be 'highly experienced', I take this to mean skills have become endorsed onto his or her professional competence repertoire.

Just as there is a need to develop and endorse appropriate professional skills, we may find on occasion we have to erase skills which are no longer applicable to sound patient care, nor indeed helpful ways of competent coping. For example, the caregivers who concentrate solely upon a disease in a patient to administer care to rather than the person who has a disease, should erase this approach and develop person-centred perceptions of health care. Retraining might be necessary to bring new skills consistent with patient-centred care into practice. Failure to erase redundant perceptions and health care practices may be met with conflicting demands from professional colleagues and lead to stressful appraisals which are difficult to cope with. Behavioural interventions in the health care professions therefore can also aid coping efforts enlisting the development and acquisition of appropriate new skills and the erasure of redundant perceptions along with antiquated modes of health care practice.

Regulating Emotions

Dynamic self-regulation of unwanted emotions is an excellent intervention against stress. When feelings of anxiety or anger well-up inside health professionals during crisis intervention work with different patient groups, both carer and patient can be adversely affected. Obvious candidates for regulating emotions are those workers in mental handicap, medical nursing, intensive care medicine/nursing, paediatrics, emergency wards, psychiatry, and rehabilitation medicine psychiatry. Nurses often stifle their emotions during a crisis only to find that after the stress-inducing incident is over they have 'buried' their feelings. Stress-regulation procedures can be used to release these feelings and restore healthier functioning to the individual.

Emotions may also be regulated before going to a predictably harrowing work period. Here a wide range of practices for managing stress should be made available to nurses and others in the field of health care provision. Examples include general relaxation procedures, systematic desensitization, autogenic regulation training, and breathing exercises. These procedures for managing stress and regulating emotions have been shown to have short- and long-term benefits. Stress control practices can benefit patients directly, and research suggests, indirectly, by benefitting health professionals such as nurses (Bailey 1983b, 1984a; Charlesworth et al. 1981). The regulation of emotions is of prime importance for caregivers if they are to optimize their professional effectiveness.

PALLIATIVE COPING

Many attempts at regulating the emotions may also involve engaging in palliative coping. Palliative coping leaves the origins or the source of stress unchanged, but it often makes us feel better — at least temporarily. For instance, using humour to deal with highly stressful encounters of intensive care nursing (Hay & Oken 1972) is one application of palliative coping which may help to overcome the otherwise overwhelming demands of caring for seriously ill patients. This is perhaps even more evident in surgical critical care units where patients are unconscious and may also have to receive treatments such as organ transplants (Gunther 1977).

Other forms of palliative coping which may be helpful in reducing intense painful emotions may come from group support — encouraging denial of professional problems. In this case defence mechanisms such as denial, detachment, projection, suppression, or intellectualization, can be enlisted to continue with the job of providing care. Similar situations can crop up in the remedial therapies and radiography and the demands made on tutorial and teaching personnel are dealt with in a similar way. Yet there seems to be a limit to the efficacy of these forms of defensive coping.

Assessing the value of palliative coping we should take into consideration the long-term effects on our functioning and on our own health and its relationship to patient care. We should also remember that palliative coping is just one aspect of more complex and interrelated forms of coping. So we would do well to investigate our own patients' other forms of coping such as defensive coping, problem-solving and emotional processing and how other health professionals regulate their emotions.

It is worthwhile being vigilant and examining when palliative coping is an effective form of coping and when it is not. This seems imperative not only for ourselves as health professionals but also for the influence it may have on patient care. We can and should help patients investigating their use of problem-solving and emotional processing use of palliative coping to regulate their emotions. Imagine this situation: A nurse and a doctor who are in daily contact with death, dying and a patient and relatives in considerable distress, find it effective when they deny or professionally distance themselves from the stressfulness of their appraisals of these circumstances. But, continued use of denial or detachments can dull their sensitivities to the patient's needs. In such a case systematic monitoring and regular assessments of palliative coping require to be made (Lazarus 1981). (E.g., using palliative coping is not in itself undesirable or desirable.) The point is to monitor and evaluate in each instance when palliative coping may be efficacious or not for the health professional and those in their care and when problem-solving skills as a form of coping may be more appropriate.

Forms of palliative coping which are also likely to bring short-term relief may have serious long-term effects on the health professional's psychological and physical health. For example, we have seen the terrible toll which smoking, long-term excessive alcohol consumption and self-prescribing of drugs has taken on the lives of doctors and their families. It is reasonable to speculate that the pronounced stress states we know as burn-out may also be heralded by injudicious forms of palliative coping. It is incumbent upon us to start making more careful and systematic stress and coping audits of ourselves. These should involve identifying those areas in ourselves and our colleagues in the health professions which reveal efficacious coping and those which do not. This is not with a view to reprimanding palliative coping efforts or penalizing those engaged in the health professions. No, it is for far more important reasons.

First, we have a responsibility to patients and client groups. Second, and by far the most neglected irony of health care, we have a responsibility — even a moral imperative — to care for each other. Humanizing health care for patients and client groups is surely a justifiable goal for all health professionals. Humanizing health care for the health professionals themselves has, however, been regrettably omitted in the development of human health welfare services (Bailey 1981, 1982a). It is time we put this matter right. A programme of health professional consultation services is now beginning to explore ways in which this can be done with nurses (Baldwin 1983). No full evaluation of these services is yet available. But, one major concern for all of us will be to research and evaluate the role of all kinds of palliative coping as a means of helping and regulating health professionals' stress and its relationships to the delivery of health care services.

Collective Coping

Collective coping may also be adopted to deal with stress and excessive work demands. Collective coping is created within those informal and formal networks of social resources that the health professional can engage or be engaged by, to mediate the impact of health care demands and stress at work. Examples of the informal networks are those which may take place during 'coffee-talk', 'tea-talk' and parties. These often function as a 'buffer' to excessive work demands and often provide opportunities for gossiping, mutual moaning and general ventilation of feelings (House 1981). The more formal social resources networks are often more explicitly aimed at collective coping to alter the meaning of professional demands, behaviour and regulation of emotions.

Research is still in its infancy in this complex and complicated area. Some health professionals, however, have also set up formal groups to facilitate health professionals' development of more effective coping. The formal arrangements for collective coping usually involve providing a service where health professionals can meet individually or in groups with an individual counsellor or stress and coping specialist. This can be as sophisticated as the establishment of a counselling service (Annandale-Steiner 1979a, 1979b; Hugill 1975) or a comprehensive nurse-consultation service (Baldwin 1983). This service can offer 'drop-in' facilities for short-term and long-term counselling.

Other options that may be taken up are stress management training (Bailey 1981, 1983a, 1983b, 1984a, 1984b). Similar to the informal activities, discussion along problem-solving lines, conflict resolution and group-griping may characterize much of the coping activity in these sessions.

Denial may also be used to overcome issues which are for the moment unbearable to talk about or express feelings directly. This can have a productive influence in distancing the health professional from the source of stress. It may also mediate in such a way that no stress is experienced by the nurse or allied health professional. Denial can play a positive role in achieving, and maintaining, detachment from stress and its sources (Barton 1977a, 1977b; Lazarus 1983a, 1983b). But, *prolonged* utilization of denial is also likely to prove counterproductive as a means of coping with stress. So caution would seem to be called for when collective coping efforts encourage the use of denial. This would seem to be the case for any attempts at coping which entail the employment of denial. The point is not whether denial should be used or not but whether and when denial should be encouraged, maintained or dismissed. Also, any individual or social resource networks which are operating should always take into consideration the possible effects on patients as well as the current state of health professional functioning. These are complex issues which are receiving more attention in stress and coping research (Lazarus 1983). For the clinical-practitioner in the health care field, they are none the less important.

Practical problems are not likely to end for the health professions simply because they have informal and formalized networks of social support whose implicit or explicit purpose is to effect collective coping. You can probably appreciate this from your own experience already. So I am not saying anything new in this respect. But, examining demands, stress and coping with the flow-model in Figure 1 you may be able to identify how collective coping may be adaptive or maladaptive at various points for the health professional and those for whom they provide care.

Because a network of collective coping opportunities exists does not mean that nurses or other health professionals will take advantage of it. Engagement with the sources of collective coping seems necessary. At the informal level this may happen incidentally. On the formal side, resistance may have to be overcome on behalf of health professionals who may be experiencing difficulties but do not see formal facilities for health professionals as necessary or useful for them or their patients. Present informal arrangements for collective coping organized only for health professional stress may alienate those who are functioning well.

It is more positive to present formalized collective coping facilities as a spectrum of consultation service for *all* health professionals whether struggling under stress or functioning healthily.

The Stanford University Hospital nurse consultation service has identified main goals, and facility functions to enhance social support and collective coping. Illustrating these as goal and facility functions should look similar to Figure 2.

Goals		Facility	
1	Promote and strengthen role performance	1	One-time consultations
2	Confidential listening	2	Long-term consultations
3	Problem-solving proficiency	3	Individual consultations
4	Resolution of intra- and inter-professional conflict (e.g. nurse-nurse, nurse-doctor)	4	Group support options
5	Promoting and maintaining well-being	5	Workshops on stress, coping and burn-out

Fig. 2 Nursing consultation service

The services shown in Figure 2 are available to all nurse personnel. Such a development would be welcomed in the UK. But it may be more appropriate to widen its appeal to include a wider range of health professionals such as doctors, remedial therapists, radiographers, medical social workers, and administrators. Central to the provision of a health consultation and counselling service for health professions should be the availability of problem-focussed coping training (Krumboltz & Thoreson 1976). But, perhaps more so, there should be included in the facility a diverse range of emotion-focussed coping procedures to help health professionals manage stress better. All health caregivers should not only utilize available help and staff support systems but also learn to control their stress.

THE PRACTICAL PERSPECTIVE

In practice you will probably recognize that we often use some combination of: altered meaning of demands; problem-focussed coping; regulation of emotions; collective coping, and defensive coping strategies for dealing with the demands of caring. We may also use *different* forms of defence mechanisms at times. It is still undetermined, however, as to when we should use denial and detachment or intellectualization or other defence mechanisms where it seems appropriate — if at all. These questions involve ethical judgements as well as further research. In terms of coping options, however, it is clear that many health professionals may use defensive coping to avoid and prevent or overcome stress. In practice, we would expect many of the appropriate professional behavioural skills to be made available to the individual health professional. However, the nursing literature medical stress reports are a reliable basis for making a more general point. They suggest that the regulation of emotions and the use of altered meaning of work demands are areas of deep concern.

As Briggs (HMSO 1972) noted it is not the routine skills which require to be taught; it is how to deal with the often unexpected, and sometimes catastrophic, demands of providing care for others which must be tackled. This can be combatted by preventing undue stress or restoring psychobiological equilibrium to the health carer. One way is to assimilate and practise techniques regulating the emotions and promoting altered meaning of health care demands, in addition to developing and endorsing new behavioural skills aimed at enhancing professional competence in general. We can begin to control stress in ourselves and other health professionals by initiating practices which involve us in dynamic self-regulation.

CHAPTER FOUR

CONTROLLING STRESS

A number of specific stress-control techniques have been developed to increase coping and enhance control over stress. Their main principle is the development of control over the involuntary sympathetic nervous system through the influence of the central nervous system and extending to the somatic functioning of the body (Schwartz 1978). These techniques come under the broad title of 'mental training'.

Much mental training involves muscle-tension relaxation and practitioners talking to themselves 'internally' and allowing their imagination and thoughts to act on the body and the mind (Schultz & Luthe 1969; Luthe 1963; Luthe & Blumberger 1977; Rosa 1976). Other approaches are concerned with allowing thoughts that are held about threatening situations to be corrected or altered. The outcomes of mental training when applied systematically have shown that behaviour and emotions can be changed (Beck 1976; Zastrow 1979; Meichenbaum 1979). People can learn to let the body and mind relax together in a natural way. This seems to produce the rest principle inherent in each human organism. Mental training and related methods help to bring it about.

Walter Hess was probably the first person to demonstrate experimentally an organism's natural rest response (Hess 1957). This was first done by using cats in his experiments. Stimulating the hypothalamus Hess found it could produce what he terms *trophotropic activity* — a rest and restorative response. The hypothalamus, regarded as an important mechanism governing the fight-flight response, was also capable of producing processes leading to restorative equilibrium in the organism. The implications for health care, and health care-givers would be clinically significant if similar activity could be produced in humans. Could it be that the hypothalamus — the stress alarm system — would also produce restorative activity in people? In other words, could the stress alarm centre also have the function of being a healing centre as well?

Later research and clinical work (Schultz & Luthe 1969; Luthe 1963; Lindemann 1974; Rosa 1976) all seem to uphold the view that this naturally restorative response is also present in the human species. (However, the mechanisms responsible for the restorative response are not yet fully understood.) It can be invoked by the practice of mental training methods. Practi-tioners often report varying degrees of relaxation and an increase in their general well-being as a result of effective training. The psychological name now given to these comfortable states and the feelings they engender in students of mental training is The Relaxation Response (Benson 1980).

There are many ways of achieving the relaxation response which may give us more control over stress. Five methods in popular use are:

1   Progressive Relaxation (PR)
2   Systematic Desensitization (SD)
3   Transcendental Meditation (TM)
4   Autogenic Regulation Training (ART)
5   Stress Innoculation Training (SIT)

PROGRESSIVE RELAXATION

Progressive relaxation (PR) techniques involve tensing and relaxing different sets of muscles in the body (Jacobson 1929, 1934). It is carried out systematically — hence progressive relaxation. Attention is also brought to the practice of breathing awareness. Relaxation training proceeds through each suc-cessive step until the practitioner begins to report feelings of relaxation, comfort, calm, rest, peacefulness, and other indi-cators that the relaxation response is present (Benson 1980).

Physiological signs of rest accompanying the relaxation response are often reflected in lower respiration rate, galvanic skin response (GSR), heart rate, and blood pressure (Benson et al. 1974; Bloomfield et al. 1975).

During PR practice any reported discomfort is a signal which should generally be taken to terminate the relaxation session. When this happens, it is often useful to return to a previous part of the practice which was pleasant, and complete relaxation training for the day at this point. It is clinically helpful too for the practitioner to end each session in a comfortable state rather than attempting to cover all of the training exercises within a fixed time period. Our commonsense and research on psychological individual differences of humans tells us that each person may relax at his or her own particular rate. In my view this suggests that just as we learn to achieve various goals in our lives, we can learn to relax. Although we may learn to relax at our own tempo, the basic technique procedures should be the same for all practitioners of this method for controlling stress.

The Method

GENERAL REQUIREMENTS

In general PR training should be conducted at least twice per day: once in the morning, and once at night immediately after retiring to bed. Afternoon sessions can be substituted for the morning session or added on to make 3 sessions of PR per day. However, not all stress problems requiring relaxation need sessions 3 times each day. Another point here is that although the patient might have time for several sessions each day, the health professional may not. My own research tends to confirm this latter point (Bailey 1984a).No food should be consumed immediately prior to stress control practice periods.

SETTING CONDITIONS

1 Find a quiet spot where you are unlikely to be disturbed.

2   Then decide upon a comfortable position to sit or lie down (a bed, couch, favourite chair or any other position where your body is supported and not strained). Use cushions or blankets for support of muscles.

3   Make sure that the place where you are to practise is not too hot or cold.

4   Now loosen any restrictive clothing such as belts, bras, collars, headgear, and shoes.

5   Do a final check on your body. Make sure ankles, calves, thighs, pelvic region, back, hands, lower arms, upper arms, shoulders, neck, and head are all supported by cushions, pillow or floor. Use the check-list shown in Figure 3.

	Supported	
	Yes	No
Head		
Neck		
Shoulders		
Lower and Upper Arms		
Hands		
Back		
Pelvic Region		
Thighs		
Calves		
Ankles and Feet		

Fig. 3   Posture-relaxation checklist. Check that each part of your body is supported.

6   Practise for a minimum of 10 minutes and a maximum of 20 for each training period. Set this period as essential, and keep a clock at hand. Glance at it when you feel the practice period is

over. Do not set an alarm as this will interfere with the development and effectiveness of progressive relaxation. Now practise the following relaxation–antistress procedure.

PROCEDURE

1 With each movement slowly count to 5, hold the muscle stretch for about 5–10 seconds. Observe a steady and rhythmic inhalation and exhalation.

2 Direct your attention to both feet, now bend your toes down away from your body. Feel the tension until it is 'tight', slowly return the toes to their normal position, pause and feel the sensations of rest in your toes.

3 Carry out the same procedure for the feet, but this time stretch the feet upwards and towards the body. Again, slowly stretch to a count of 5, hold for 5–10 seconds and gradually rest to stopping point. Feel the sensations and accept them.

4 Continue moving to the calves. Carry out a forward calf stretch, hold, relax, and appreciate the sensations of rest and relaxation.

5 Again stretch the calves, hold, relax using the same procedure this time with the backward movement. Remember to bend to the point where the tension is tight. Hold your calves in this position and gradually let go. Relax and enjoy the sensations you are now feeling.

6 Now stiffen and tighten your thigh muscles. Relax them in the same way. Gradually sense the growing warmth and spreading relaxation in your body.

7 Move to your buttocks. Tense them until tight — then gradually relax them. Accept and appreciate the release of tension.

8 Now tense both of your fists and arms so tight they vibrate. Slowly release the tension, becoming aware of any warmth, heaviness and general feeling of well-being.

9 Let your attention move to your neck and back muscles. Draw them in until they are bearably 'hard'. Then after a few seconds, 'let go'. Allow this muscle group to find their own posi-

tion of rest. Now relax and enjoy the release of tension in this area of your body.

10   Next 'screw up' all the muscles of the face; around the mouth, eyes, nose, and forehead. Hold this position between 5 and 10 seconds and then allow all of your face muscles to return to their natural resting position. Feel the relaxation and any 'glow' from the aftermath of this exercise.

11   Now link up all of the exercises you have done by tensing all of the groups of muscles together. Hold the tension then gradually release — allow the complete feeling of relaxation to permeate the whole of your body.

12   Finally, imagine a pulsing ball of energy gradually and systematically travelling throughout all of the areas of your body you have relaxed. Feel how this energy ball, your life-force, brings with it a sense of oneness and lightness in a state of comfortable calmness. Stay with this feeling of complete ease, and allow it to link up with all of your body so that you are now bathed in total relaxation. Your relaxation training session is now completed. Each session should be followed by a cancellation procedure.

CANCELLATION

Cancellation of progressive relaxation should be done by opening the eyes and making slow but deliberate movements of the body. No attempts should be made deliberately to tense and relax the muscles again. When the muscle tone has returned to your limbs, neck and face, you can stand up. After standing, take one or two deep breaths, let your breathing carry on as it usually does. When the cancellation has been effected, you can take up any task which requires your attention.

Cancellation *must* be carried out in order to achieve alertness. Failure to cancel your relaxed state is not intrinsically a problem, but it may leave you feeling lethargic. If this happens, provided you do not have to carry out any tasks which demand close, clear attention, cancellation presents no difficulty. But, when you are likely to be preparing for a work period, it is unwise not to cancel the effects of the relaxation procedure.

The only time cancellation can be usefully omitted is when practising progressive relaxation in bed at night shortly before going to sleep. Cancellation can be carried out when you awaken next morning, by opening your eyes, stretching and taking a few deep breaths. This is quite natural and largely mirrors what we do after a prolonged period of restful sleep whether or not we are practising relaxation training.

SYSTEMATIC DESENSITIZATION

A system of combining progressive relaxation with systematic desensitization was developed by an American psychologist, Joseph Wolpe (1958–1973). This system of stress control is helpful for dealing with specific stress reactions such as anxiety and phobias. Arnold Lazarus, a researcher in applied psychology, has also shown that the assumptions underlying this approach to stress control are physiological and cognitive as well as behavioural. People with specific stress reactions are 'sensitized' to various situations or stimuli (Wolpe 1958; Wolpe & Lazarus 1966; Lazarus A. 1972, 1976).

The sensitization results in an increase in physiological arousal activity in the nervous system which is often coupled with a release of increased adrenalin, a stress hormone associated with different states of anxiety and reported fear (Wittkower & Warnes 1977). Sensitization is also influenced by the way a person appraises situations or stimuli (Lazarus 1966, 1976, 1981; Lazarus & Launier 1978). For instance, a situation such as being asked to prepare a patient for surgery is a stress-inducing threat which takes the form of increased adrenalin flow, and reported anxiety. So physiological activity is also 'triggered' by the way a person views demands from the environment. It could also have been that preparing a patient for surgery would now receive 'correct treatment'.

Therefore, thinking, or more properly *cognition* (Meichenbaum 1979; Neisser 1972) — which includes memory, meaning, thinking — influences the presence or absence of experienced stress and different levels of physiological activity. The way the nurse and other health professionals 'see' situations and what they think about their work demands, therefore, is important in two respects. First, changing the way health caregivers think about the demands made upon them will change the threat-potency of the demands from their environment. Second, when a stress-inducing threat is overcome, this should be seen as a transfer from having little control to a reported increase in control over previously stress-inducing threats. You will be able to remain calm and composed in the face of situations or stimuli which you previously appraised as harmful, and consequently experienced anxiety, anger, depression, or fear. The same may be said for patients.

A TYPICAL PROCEDURE

The aim of this approach to stress control is quite specific. You and other professionals should have, as your goal, a state of relaxation and rational composure in the face of a previously disturbing or upsetting situation. Therefore, the first task is to identify and define precisely what it is that induces the threat and stress reaction. After this, practise desensitization with progressive relaxation.

Practice can be done using the typical protocol shown in the preceding section, or some other procedure which permits the individual to achieve a comfortable and relaxed state throughout the mind and body. When the relaxation response can be achieved quite regularly and without great difficulty, you can then begin to desensitize yourself to identified threatening situations. Desensitization may be carried out in the imagination (Wolpe 1958, 1973; Bakal 1979) or where and when the threat actually occurs (in vivo).

Many studies of systematic desensitization suggest that in vivo practice is more effective than imaginative desensitization (Lazarus A. 1976). However, both procedures are often therapeutic. Selection of one or the other should depend on the nature of the threat, and the imaginative ability of the person to be

desensitized. Before actually starting the desensitization
sessions, the individual should draw up a hierarchy of situations,
and their threat potency. This is a central component of systematic desensitization and should be constructed very carefully. If
you require desensitization to any threat, e.g., panic attacks
when asked to carry out Last Offices, a trained counsellor or
tutor could help you to draw up the panic hierarchy. Finally, you
should reach agreement about what signs to use if psychological
discomfort is experienced during the stress-control period. If you
carry out desensitization programmes on yourself, care should
be taken to ensure that adequate relaxation training has been
established prior to attempts at desensitization. A desensitization protocol for use with a nurse's phobic fear of blood, and
satisfactory stress control over this threat illustrates the
procedure.

Protocol 13

Specific Source of Threat: The sight or thought of blood.
    Nurse's appraisal of this situation (at the thought of it or
when it occurs): 'Oh No! Not again. I feel tense and queasy. I
think I am going to faint.'
    Preparation: The nurse was prepared for desensitization
by attending a well-nurse clinic (Bailey 1981). The clinic ran
classes to show nurses how to practise progressive relaxation.
The blood-phobic nurse practised progressive relaxation for
four weeks until the relaxation response was established.
During this time she was asked to prepare a blood-phobia hierarchy. Six situations of increasing threat were identified, and
marked for the degree of fear experienced. The blood-phobia
hierarchy could then be drawn up (see Fig. 4).
    The threat-fear profile in Figure 4 shows where the nurse's
coping control over 'blood' threat is manageable and breaks
down. Low threat induces little fear, and in this case, she can
manage the threat of blood with some discomfort. As the threats
move up the hierarchy from the 'thought of blood' to 'blood seen
on emergency admissions', there is an increase in experienced

Situations

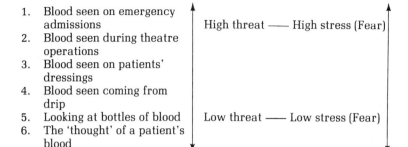

1. Blood seen on emergency
   admissions
2. Blood seen during theatre
   operations
3. Blood seen on patients'
   dressings
4. Blood seen coming from
   drip
5. Looking at bottles of blood
6. The 'thought' of a patient's
   blood

High threat —— High stress (Fear)

Low threat —— Low stress (Fear)

Fig. 4 Blood-phobia hierarchy.

fear. At the high fear point, this nurse found she panicked because of the unmanageable level of psychophysiological fear. The blood-fear hierarchy must be completed before proceeding with combined relaxation-desensitization as a means of stress control. Doing this provides a baseline measurement of the nurse's stress reaction to threat. Put another way, baseline measurements should be taken to compare the efficacy of any stress-control interventions. More will be said about baseline measures later in this chapter.

PRACTISING STRESS CONTROL

When the baseline measurement of the phobia hierarchy is complete and relaxation established, the nurse had adequately prepared for practising relaxation with systematic desensitization. Practice continued by combining the state of relaxation produced in progressive relaxation with gradual exposure to the threats listed by the nurse in the blood-phobia hierarchy. In this case I asked the nurse to 'prepare' herself to deal with these threats connected with actual experience and thoughts of blood. The background to the reported fears was explained to her in the following way:

'We all have fears. Some are essential for our everyday survival such as fear of going without food, water or shelter for an unusually long period of time. But, there are fears which are not helpful to our survival, such as fear of breathing and of open or closed spaces. These fears may be so great that they interfere with our work and personal life. Most fears are learned. A person learns to fear things because they are seen as threatening. But, just as we learn to fear things we find threatening, we can also learn to relax and be calm in the face of threats. When this is done, situations lose their threatening significance or 'threat potency'. Your fears can be changed in the same way. We shall now use a procedure called combined relaxation-systematic desensitization to reduce the fear you experience from the threatening situations you have described.'

1   The nurse practises progressive relaxation and establishes the relaxation response. This is indicated by physiological and psychological measures showing a change of state. The practitioner may say 'I'm relaxed; calm; at peace; I feel good; etc.' Alternatively the practitioner may be asked to press a button lighting a green light for 'relaxed state achieved'. A press button which produces a red light can be used when the practitioner wishes to 'stop the procedure'.

2   Once the relaxed state is regularly achieved, the least threatening item of the hierarchy is presented (in this case, thought of blood). The nurse is asked to think about the colour of blood, how blood is composed and its functions. Finally, in this instance, the nurse was told to imagine as clearly as possible how blood was central to the many tasks she carried out at work. In a matter of fact way, she was asked to imagine continuing her work despite any thoughts connected with blood. This part of the hierarchy was carried out for one week with the nurse indicating complete relaxation midway through the third session. This was the signal to continue up the hierarchy.

3   Sessions continued for a period of 8 weeks, 5 days per week, using the same approach. Relaxation established; then

practising the ideas of seeing the items from the threat hierarchy and feeling calm.

4   All of the threats on the hierarchy were submitted to this procedure. When the nurse continued to feel relaxed, and no longer saw the blood hierarchy as threatening, stress-control training was terminated.

The results were then recorded. Then they were compared with the baseline measure of the threat-stress hierarchy. You can see how effective this stress-control procedure has been with the nurse (Fig. 5).

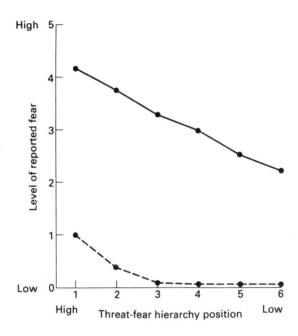

Fig. 5   Threat-fear hierarchy. The continuous line shows the base-line level of reported fear, and the broken line shows the level of reported fear after practising stress control.

EFFECTS OF DESENSITIZATION FOR BLOOD
PHOBIA

From a comparison, we find that only one threat remained which
induced a modicum of fear. This was the threat of seeing blood in
emergency admissions. But now the intensity of the threat has
come to the bottom of the threat hierarchy and it induces only a
very low level of fear. Further practice sessions actually carried
out during emergency admissions are likely to remove this final
threat.

Protocol 14

A similar approach to removing an excessive fear of blood in a
nurse has been reported in a case study by Max Rardin (1969).
This case characterized the problem experienced by the nurse
as one of haemophobia, an 'incapacitating fear of blood'. It was
treated by a variation of the desensitization technique developed
by Joseph Wolpe, a fear hierarchy and progressive relaxation.
The decision to approach the problem in this way was based on a
history of the case and clinical data gathered by the
psychologist.

The subject, a woman, was an 18-year-old nurse student, in
the first year of her nursing education programme, see Rardin
(1969). This case showed quite clearly the prominent threatening
significance blood had for the nurse student. The particularly
pressing concern for her proficiency as a nurse, and caring for
patients, was her reactions to the threat of blood. It is evident in
this case, that it impaired her personal control over a range of
imagined and actual situations associated with blood, inducing a
number of stressful reactions. Rardin reports the following
history of events:

'The client indicated that she had been fearful of blood and
generally squeamish for several years but her fears had not been
serious concern until she entered nursing — a career goal for
her since childhood. . . .

'. . . Her reaction to blood and possible physical injury varied from moderate discomfort to dizziness and nausea depending on the topic and circumstances. The immediate concern was her reaction to the film shown in nursing classes which vividly depicted various medical conditions. On a number of occasions, she had to put her head down or leave the room. She felt she would faint or vomit if she continued to observe the film [p. 125].'

These reactions interfered so much with her nurse student performance in the classes with films that the nursing faculty began to question her suitability for the profession. At this point, the nurse student, with the encouragement of her tutors, contacted a clinical psychologist about 'the possibility of *controlling* her fear of blood' [emphasis mine].

Like Protocol 13, a preparation and a practice period for stress control was adopted as the therapeutic strategy:

1   The nurse student was given a detailed description of relaxation-desensitization and how it would be applied in her situation.
2   Three sessions were then devoted to the practice of relaxation training.
3   A fear hierarchy was constructed.

The fear hierarchy consisted of the 16 items listed. They involved increasing *amounts* of blood appearing due to injury, surgery and childbirth. Relaxation and vivid imagery established, she began to become desensitized to the fear hierarchy items. By the end of the nursing school term, 7 of the 16 following fear items had successfully been desensitized.

1   Bleeding from nose and mouth due to internal injury
2   A 'sucking' chest wound
3   Seeing a blood sample drawn
4   Blood pouring from the mouth
5   Waters breaking from childbirth
6   Head emerging during childbirth and effect on mother
7   Blood flowing after birth
8   Delivery of placenta

   9   Stitching after delivery
10   Scraped elbow*
11   A torn hangnail*
12   Squeezing out one drop of blood*
13   A cut in the sole of the foot*
14   A compound fracture of the leg*
15   Needle in the skin for a stitch*
16   Gash in the arm with flowing blood*

Starred items were successfully desensitized by the end of the nursing term. The remaining threats in the fear hierarchy were dealt with by the nurse with self-administered desensitization at home. Using a monologue prepared by the psychologist, she practised relaxation-desensitization 5 or 6 nights a week for a period of 6 weeks. This was found to be effective at home and generalized to actual events occurring at work.

'At the end of 6 weeks she contacted the author and reported being able to imagine comfortably all of the items on the list and having visited the hospital maternity ward. She was too late for the delivery but did see the cord being cut and the delivery of the placenta. At that point she felt faint and left. She then requested that she be allowed to use smelling salts at her next birth observation since her dizziness was not accompanied by nausea.

'Because she attributed this faintness more to excitement than anxiety, she was given permission to use smelling salts with the condition that she should not force herself to observe if she felt highly anxious. She observed her next delivery successfully. The last session occurred after her return to school and was primarily a review of events to complete the case history [p. 126].'

During this closing session, she reported 'having observed a complete delivery, successfully taken blood samples, and having her own blood sample taken. One year later she was on an obstetric ward assisting in deliveries to the point of dabbing blood between vaginal stitches.'

Practising Relaxation-desensitization

SUMMARY

Protocols 13 and 14 serve to illustrate how a common incapacitating fear — haemophobia — can be brought under effective control. They also emphasize that baseline measures should be made before stress control practices are initiated. More generally, it can be seen from both studies how the individual may be educated to practise stress control procedures personally and reduce dependency on relaxation-desensitization sessions held in stress control clinics.

Promoting the management of stress by combined relaxation-desensitization, largely helps the practitioner to gain personal control over threatening situations by counterconditioning (Wolpe & Lazarus 1966). Whereas previously threats in the blood phobia hierarchy had conditioned the nurse to be sensitized, pairing relaxation with each step of the hierarchy reconditioned her to relax. This process is called *reciprocal inhibitions* (Wolpe 1958). The relaxation response inhibits the physiological and psychological responses associated with fear, anxiety and other stress reactions.

PROCEDURE

1   Practise progressive relaxation. Establish the production of the relaxation response.

2   Draw up a threat hierarchy and measure the stress response associated with each threat. Record these in written and graphic form.

3   Begin systematic desensitization by relaxing and comparing the first step on the threat hierarchy with your relaxation state. Be sure to progress up the threat hierarchy at the practitioner's pace. When there is any indication of some discomfort or loss of relaxation at any item on the threat hierarchy, you should return to a lower level of threat where relaxation can be re-established. Stress control sessions should always end

with the practitioner reporting a calm composed state.

4   Continue practising the procedure until all the items on the threat hierarchy can be managed, and relaxation is established regularly.

5   Record any changes in threat-stress reactions during the stress control sessions.

6   Terminate stress control sessions when the stress reactions originally reported and measured (e.g., anxiety, fear, heart rate) have reached a comfortable level.

7   Compare any changes in threat and reported stress reactions with the baseline measures taken prior to stress control training.

Combining relaxation with systematic desensitization should permit you to practise stress control for a variety of specific problems. This form of stress control is best used where the threats to you are identifiable, and the stress reactions, specific e.g., fear, anxiety, anger. When a general and diffuse lack of well-being is evident across a wide range of professional demands, a broader stress control practice such as meditation would seem more appropriate.

MEDITATION

Meditation is not easy to define. One who meditates is as often regarded as 'exercising the mind', or 'contemplating'. Though the act of meditating often relies on exercising the mind in a contemplative manner, the experience of meditation is not an awareness of contemplation, or dwelling on a subject. People who regularly meditate, report being calm, composed and, paradoxically, relaxed and alert at the same time. So meditation involves an act which, when one is in the meditative state, is an individual experience of being. The different experiences of being are then reported as 'feelings of calm', 'at rest with myself', 'at peace' and statements of well-being.

How is the meditative state achieved? What typical practices are carried out by the individual to induce the meditative state reported by meditators as different feelings of well-being? Two Eastern approaches which have been internalized into Western practice have come from Hindu philosophy and the practice of meditation. The Hindu Sanskrit words for these methods are *Yantra* and *Mantra* meditation (Petersen 1979; Wood 1969).

Yantra Meditation

When Yantra meditation is practised, you adopt a visual image like a candle or abstract shape to dispel intrusive thoughts from the mind. The main object of the Yantra is to permit you to enter the meditative state. Typically, Yantra meditation entails sitting cross-legged or in some other comfortable position such as in an armchair in a quiet room, and attending to the visual image. You should not stare but merely gaze at the candle or other visual image and accept the thoughts which come and allow them to pass from awareness. Once these thoughts have been allowed to pass away you will have enabled them to be expelled naturally from your mind. Just as a cloud drifts across the sun, allow your thoughts to drift by and allow your mind to become bright and clear. As this happens, clearness of thought, tranquillity and heightened awareness of the self, and others, is often reported. When intrusive thoughts occur, attention to the natural rhythm of breathing should help you dispel any occasional interferences with the production of the meditative state. Sometimes simple awareness of your breath (Ramachakara 1974) may be enough to overcome intrusions such as an excess of worrying thoughts. Preparation and practice of Yantra meditation may take the following form.

PREPARATION

1   You should not have any serious medical condition likely to be aggravated by Yantra practice (e.g., extremely low blood pressure).

2   It should be possible for you to produce the Yantra image of meditation when the eyes are closed. However, you should estab-

lish a satisfactory image by looking first at the Yantra, e.g., candle, spiral, or reversing figure, before producing it by visual imagining on its own.

3 A suitable posture should be adopted. By 'suitable' is meant practical and comfortable, e.g., sitting on the floor cross-legged, sitting comfortably upright in an armchair or other positions which do not put a strain on the back.

4 Prepare by visualizing the image by opening and closing your eyes until the image can be produced quite readily when the eyes are resting in their half-open or closed position.

PRACTICE

When the Yantra image can be produced frequently by you, preparation should then be sufficient to practise Yantra meditation. The procedure shown here is necessarily a short one, but it is adequate for you to establish at least some degree of relaxation during the Yantra meditation period.

PROCEDURE

1 Establish the Yantra image.

2 Look at the image until your eyes naturally start to close.

3 Maintain the image on closing or half-closing the eyes.

4 When the image disappears, reopen the eyes enough to establish it again. Relax the eyelids, maintaining the Yantra image.

5 A candle is a common Yantra image. If you have adopted it, see how the details of the candle begin to appear in sharp clarity. Note for instance its form, colour, ever-changing shape, whether it has a momentum, a 'dancing flame' or 'motionless spear of light'. Any other features which may occur to you such as observations of the wax and wick stem should be acknowledged but not thought about.

6 Practise this meditation for 10–20 minutes at least twice a day.

7   Do not try to force the Yantra images or what you desire to 'see' during the meditation. It is against the meditational process at this level of Yantra practice (Petersen 1979).

Mantra Meditation

Sometimes the student of meditation cannot establish the visual images required for Yantra meditation. Indeed, many meditators prefer Mantra meditation which deals with sounds and phrases rather than visual mental images. It is usual for the Mantra meditator to be given a secret word or phrase by a tutor or guide in meditation. This sound or set of sounds is then designed as the Mantra for that person.

Preparation similar to that in the Yantra meditation is made, except that in Mantra meditation, you practise by reciting the given Mantra continuously. It is also beneficial to harmonize the Mantra. This can be done by synchronizing the Mantra repetition with breathing in and out. Although, inhalations and exhalations should not dictate the pace at which the Mantra is uttered. Typical Mantras are 'love', 'I am at peace' and 'om'. Although Mantras are regarded as sacred, researchers such as Petersen (1979) and Benson (1980) have found nonsense syllables or simple words like 'one' and 'calm' can be used by the meditator to produce meditation and relaxation experiences. So it would seem that the Mantra need not necessarily be kept secret, or indeed sacred, to obtain the reported benefits of meditation. This is a distinct advantage, for it makes it possible for nurses, their patients and other related health professionals, to practise Mantra meditation without having to object to it on the grounds that it is against their religious beliefs.

As in Yantra meditation, some attention may be given to breath control when overintrusive thoughts are present. However, repetition of the Mantra is usually sufficient to dispel such interference. Preparation for the Mantra should also precede practice.

PREPARATION

1   Establish a comfortable sitting position.

2   Choose a time for meditation when there will be no interruption.

3   Do a 'body check' in your mind, acknowledging each set of muscles and allowing them to relax.

4   Become aware of your breathing — let it take its natural rhythmical course.

5   Say your Mantra, e.g., 'peace', with each outgoing breath; say it aloud to begin with, then silently and inwardly to yourself.

PRACTICE

1   Practise the same Mantra for each meditation period.

2   Meditation should be practised for a period of 10–20 minutes (do not exceed this length of time).

3   Continuously repeat the Mantra. This should not be as a voice inside but the thought of it. The Mantra should not be 'heard'.

4   Synchronize meditating of the Mantra with each breath.

5   When intrusive thoughts do block the meditation of the Mantra, stop the Mantra and acknowledge the presence of the intrusion for three breaths (exhalations). After this immediately return to the repetition of the Mantra. Continue until the meditation period is over.

6   Cancel the meditation by gradually becoming aware of the different parts of your body again. Slowly open your eyes and deliberately take two or three deep breaths, shake your hands, move your neck from side to side, bring your attention to the muscle tone returning to your body. Finally, notice your normal waking state and any events which may be going on around you. The meditation period is now over.

TRANSCENDENTAL MEDITATION (TM) AND THE RELAXATION RESPONSE

Mantra meditation is the basis of what is now regarded as transcendental meditation, or TM (Bloomfield *et al.* 1975). This is a simplified version of Mantra meditation brought to Western society by The Maharishi Mahesh Yogi. Experiments using a modified TM technique have been carried out by Herbert Benson and his colleagues to help hypertensive patients control and reduce high blood pressure. Using this approach, Benson suggests that TM evokes the relaxation response which is characterized by a drop in the rate of metabolic function. Characteristic features of this change are reduced systolic-diastolic blood pressures, heart rate and respiratory responses. Similar benefits can be achieved by nurses and other health professionals using this procedure for stress control. Preparation and practice of the Benson form of TM is similar to Mantra meditation.

The Benson Technique — Relaxation Response

PREPARATION

1   Find a quiet environment, e.g., room or church, where you can regularly practise your TM.

2   To save the mind from wandering, choose a word or phrase which can be repeated over and over again.

3   Let your eyes close when repeating the word or phrase (Mantra).

4   Attend to the rhythm of your breathing in tune with the utterance of the word or phrase.

5   Disregard all intrusive thoughts (they are of no importance — 'just thoughts').

6   Don't force the meditation. Adopt a 'let it happen' attitude. This passive attitude is central to the practice of all TM and can only help the elicitation of the relaxation response. You cannot 'force' yourself to relax, so just let any intrusive

thought pass through and out of your mind.

7 Make sure you have a comfortable sitting position — cross-legged, kneeling or sitting on your haunches. Test which suits you best and adopt this posture for all subsequent TM practice.

PRACTICE

1 Sit quietly in your selected position.

2 Close your eyes.

3 Now relax all of your muscles by thinking they are relaxed. Begin by attending to your ankles and feet, moving up the body to the neck, shoulders and face (see pp. 74–5).

4 Observe your breathing through your nose. Each time you breathe out say 'one'. Breathe in and out again and say 'one'. Let your breathing occur naturally, falling on the phrase word you have adopted.

5 Continue TM practice for 10–20 minutes.

6 Ignore any intrusive thoughts. Continue to say 'one' each time you breathe out.

7 Cancel the meditation practice by sitting quietly with your eyes closed. Do not repeat 'one' after each exhalation any more. Open your eyes, sit up for a few more minutes, shake your arms and legs, then stand up. The meditation period is now over.

Benefits from Meditation

The attentive reader will already have noticed a considerable degree of similarity in the preparation and practice of meditation. This is particularly evident in Mantra meditation, which the West knows as Transcendental Meditation. Some of the benefits of meditation have been demonstrated in comparative studies of meditators and non-meditators. For instance, experiments have shown that a slowing of the metabolism can be induced by meditation. This state, described as *hypometabolism*, is associated with a decrease in oxygen take-up, blood pressure, heart rate, and respiratory responses in meditators. Meditators also tend to show faster reflexes, less anxiety, fewer headaches, colds, less insomnia, and recover more quickly from anxiety-inducing films than do non-meditators. Petersen (1979) succintly summarizes the value of meditation for dealing with anxiety:

'Another benefit of meditation is that it reduces anxiety and increases your *control* over your own body and mind. Changes in the chemistry of the blood are one indication of anxiety which have been used by students. Without exception students who meditate have been shown to have less anxiety and tension than students who do not meditate [my italics, p. 10].'

Practising meditation might, therefore, seem a useful part of health professional education in the near future. For it is clear that caregiving professions have to deal with many threatening situations which induce anxiety (Bailey 1983a, 1983b; HMSO 1972). However, it may be said that nurses, in particular, have also to be alert in the care they give patients. Being alert to patient needs is at the centre of new concepts of total nursing care (Allen 1980).

So, does meditation permit the nurse to be alert at the same time as being relaxed? Paradoxical as it may sound, this seems to be the case. An experiment held at the University of Texas recorded meditators as responding 30 per cent faster and more accurately than non-meditators did to a key-pressing task (Bloomfield et al. 1975; Petersen 1979). The investigators argued that the meditators were faster and more accurate than non-meditators for two reasons. First, the meditators were in a state of 'restful alertness'. Second, the non-meditators became a little tense just before pressing the selected key, thus slowing them down compared to the students who meditated. Reporting from a background of clinical work, Bloomfield et al. (1975) and Petersen (1979) both confirm the view that meditators can develop the combination of relaxation and alertness.

'The meditator achieves a state of alertness along with relaxation. Not only do people who meditate perform during moments of crisis, but continued practice with meditation enables them to achieve a level of restful alertness at all times. Because of this fact they are able to recover more quickly from tense situations [p. 9].'

A testimony of this kind may be subject to criticism. For meditation of itself may only help the person become aware of problems and of what should be done about them. In this sense, meditation does not bring about the many efficacious results claimed in the literature. Nonetheless, the difference between meditator and non-meditators is validated by field research and clinical studies (Bloomfield et al. 1975; Goleman 1976). Moreover, the differences are attributed to the various types of meditation which are practised. More research is required on the question of meditation and its effect on individual meditators.

In the meantime, the regular practice of meditation can have considerable benefits to health professionals particularly in reducing anxiety, and promoting composed alertness in the face of occupational demands. It remains for interested investigators to research and further evaluate the place meditation and other antistress practices might have in the education of health professionals. Also of special interest will be the influence meditation and related stress control techniques could specifically have in preparing nurse learners, qualified nurses and allied professions to remain calm, cogent and competent, under the role demands they experience in their job. Studies of this kind are already underway assessing the value of autogenic regulation training (ART) as a means of stress control with nurse students (Bailey 1984a). In these studies I found favourable reductions in sickness absence for an ART group compared with higher sickness absence rates in a control group.

AUTOGENIC REGULATION TRAINING (ART)

The basic method of autogenic regulation training (ART) was devised by Dr Johannes Schultz (1959) a Berlin neurologist, and elaborated by Dr Wolfgang Luthe (1963) in Montreal, Canada. Dr Schultz noticed that his patients moved into a trophotropic or healing state when they practised giving themselves instructions to different parts of their body — particularly those parts connected with the involuntary nervous system. For example, the practitioner of autogenics can regulate the flow of blood to the hands by using phrases such as 'my arms are heavy and warm'. Reports of regulating heart rate, decreasing respiratory functioning and blood pressure, and reduced muscle tension have also been validated by research into the effects of autogenic regulation training (Schultz & Luthe 1959; Luthe 1963; Luthe & Blumberger 1977). Alpha waves — measures of one kind of electrical brain impulse associated with calmness, relaxation and well-being — seem to increase with the practice of autogenic regulation training. These brain waves are usually accompanied by individual reports of relaxation, peace, tranquillity, and well-being from those who practice ART. Generally speaking the trophotropic response generated by autogenic regulation training, seems to be psychophysiologically similar to Benson's relaxation response (Bakal 1979; Benson 1980).

Practising ART, like the meditation in the relaxation response, means adopting a passive attitude towards stress-control training. A central assumption of autogenics is that the human organism is a natural self-regulating psychophysiological system. Each individual has a natural psychobiological balance which maintains the equilibrium of organ processes and functions of the body. In biological terms, this equilibrium is called *homeostasis* (Cannon 1932). But, because stress reactions are induced by cognitive appraisal (an appraisal that 'personal harm is anticipated') it is perhaps more appropriate to refer to psychobiological homeostasis.

One implication of this restated position is that just as the body learns to react to threatening situations by anxiety, anger or sadness, so too it can learn to be calm and composed. Conversely, when a person tries to hold back those feelings, he or she can also learn to relax and 'let them go'. This can be done by a series of autogenic regulation exercises. ART exercises also involve your literally talking to different parts of your body, and giving psychological instructions of heaviness, warmth, calm, and peacefulness to yourself. Each autogenic regulation training exercise is graded, and should be tailored to the psychological progress of the practitioner. As progress with autogenic regulation training becomes evident, previously disturbing events will often lose their threatening significance and stress reactions will be less intense. Also, pent up stress is often discharged out of the body and can take different forms such as laughing, crying, sighing, warmth etc. This process has variously been called *autogenic discharge, autogenic neutralization* (Luthe & Blumberger 1977), or simply *neutralization*.

PREPARATION

The techniques employed in autogenic regulation training have been developed to promote natural self-healing by the psychophysiological systems operating in each person. The main emphasis is on removing 'blocks' to the self-regulating and restorative processes which give rise to a trophotropic state and relaxation (Luthe & Blumberger 1977; Bailey 1984a).

After some initial training in each autogenic exercise and controlled practice of ART, you can carry out antistress exercises in your own privacy, and in your own time. As with other techniques, a number of preparatory steps should first be observed.

1   You should have no medical condition such as heart disease or alcoholism which prevents you from practising ART.

2   You should have the suppport of a nurse qualified in ART or a professional colleague familiar with ART.

3   A passive concentration should be adopted towards each ART exercise.

4   The basic ideas behind ART and its practice should be explained to you.

PRACTICE

When practising ART you should pursue the antistress training exercise 3 times: first thing in the morning after getting up and out of bed, midday or early evening, and immediately before retiring for the evening. Similar consideration should be given if you are a night shift worker. Three different positions should be adopted for each time of day:

1   the simple sitting position
2   the reclining armchair position
3   the lying horizontal position

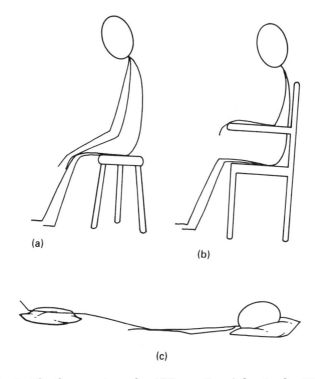

Fig. 6   The three postures for ART practice a) the simple sitting posture b) the armchair posture c) the horizontal, or lying, posture.

A passive attitude should be employed with repetition of verbal formulas which help to promote the trophotropic state. This is associated with a reduction in proprioceptive and exteroceptive stimulation (e.g., from touch, vision and hearing).

1   Regularly practise ART in a quiet place, e.g., bedroom, library, until the trophotropic state and relaxation is readily achieved. Thereafter the degree of noise or visual stimulation should not interfere with ART practice and its effects.

2   Practise ART in the morning (or at the first convenient time) in the simple sitting position.

3   ART sessions at midday or early evening should be carried out in the reclining armchair position.

4   The final ART session should be carried out in bed prior to sleep. This session should be conducted in the horizontal position. (Do not be concerned if you fall asleep during this session. You will probably have entered the trophotropic state, and cancel the state when next you wake up. This is done quite naturally by stretching your arms, legs, wriggling your toes, blinking, and taking a few deep breaths of fresh air.)

5   Repeat each exercise three times, i.e., say to yourself the formula 3 times for each position at the different times of the day.

6   Cancel each session by:

a)   clenching the fists and briskly flexing the arms back towards the shoulders

b)   taking a deep inhalation of air, and

c)   opening your eyes and blinking

The autogenic regulation training session is then over. You can stand up and carry on in your usual way, after cancelling each exercise. Remember to cancel each ART session to avoid any 'sluggishness'. Cancelling also fulfils the function of toning up the muscles and bringing your consciousness back into an alert attentiveness.

EXERCISE SCHEDULE

The following 6-week schedule is a shortened version of ART which can be practised by you and your health care colleagues. Practise the consecutive weekly exercise 3 times per day in sitting, reclining or lying horizontal position. Begin each exercise in the following way:

1 Sit quietly, close your eyes.

2 Repeat each instruction 3 times silently and rhythmically
to yourself:

ART — Week 1

My right arm is heavy	(x3)
My left arm is heavy	(x3)
Both my arms are heavy	(x3)
My right leg is heavy	(x3)
My left leg is heavy	(x3)
Both my legs are heavy	(x3)
My arms and legs are heavy	(x3)
I am Calm and at Peace	(x3)

Now cancel the exercise by clenching your fists, flexing the arms
to the shoulders; take a deep breath and open your eyes.

ART — Week 2

My right arm is heavy	(x3)
My left arm is heavy	(x3)
Both my arms are heavy	(x3)
My right leg is heavy	(x3)
My left leg is heavy	(x3)
Both my legs are heavy	(x3)
My arms and legs are heavy	(x3)
My heartbeat is regular and calm	(x3)
I am at Peace	(x3)

Now cancel the exercise by clenching your fists, flexing the arms
to the shoulders; take a deep breath and open your eyes.

ART — Week 3

My arms and legs are heavy and warm	(x3)
My heartbeat is regular and calm	(x3)
My body breathes for me	(x3)
I am at Peace	(x3)

Now cancel the exercise by clenching your fists, flexing the arms to the shoulders; take a deep breath and open your eyes.

ART — Week 4

My arms and legs are heavy and warm	(x3)
My heartbeat is regular and calm	(x3)
My body breathes for me	(x3)
My neck and shoulders are heavy and warm	(x3)
I am at Peace	(x3)

Now cancel the exercise by clenching your fists, flexing the arms to the shoulders; take a deep breath and open your eyes.

ART — Week 5

My arms and legs are heavy and warm	(x3)
My heartbeat is regular and calm	(x3)
My body breathes for me	(x3)
My neck and shoulders are heavy and warm	(x3)
My solar plexus glows warm	(x3)
I am at Peace	(x3)

Now cancel the exercise by clenching your fists, flexing the arms to the shoulders; take a deep breath and open your eyes.

ART — Week 6

My arms and legs are heavy and warm	(x3)
My heartbeat is regular and calm	(x3)
My body breathes for me	(x3)
My neck and shoulders are heavy and warm	(x3)
My solar plexus glows warm	(x3)
My forehead is cool and clear	(x3)
I am at Peace	(x3)

Now cancel the exercise by clenching your fists, flexing the arms to the shoulders; take a deep breath and open your eyes.

Changes and Benefits

Each ART exercise can be monitored for its therapeutic effects. The total autogenic regulation training period can also be assessed for its efficacy by you. This is usually best done in consultation with a supervising nurse, doctor or clinical psychologist who is familiar with ART and the range of its possible effects. Early changes from practising ART often come through your self-report and body movements. These reports can range from feelings of well-being to some initial discomfort associated with relief and the discharge of tension from the body (Schultz & Luthe 1959; Luthe & Blumberger 1977). These forms of *autogenic neutralization* of tension release are termed *autogenic discharges*. Some typical observations made by practitioners of ART can be recorded in a 'feelings list', or Practitioner's Record, for example:

Practitioner record		
Feeling observed	heaviness	tingling
and reported	warmth	floating
	twitching	pain
	happiness	anxiety
	laughter	sadness
	elation	tearfulness

The benefits of autogenic discharge, therefore, may be pleasant or discomforting or some mixture of both during autogenic regulation training. Discomforting discharges benefit you in that the brain and body work together to 'flush-out' the barriers to mutual self-regulation, and psychobiological homeostasis (Moore 1984). So, for instance, crying may precede laughter, or anxiety, happiness. There is, however, no set sequence of autogenic discharges.

Many people carrying out autogenic regulation training do not experience feelings of tension and discomfort. In general they report feelings of relaxation, peacefulness, physical and psychological well-being. A wide range of psychological and physical benefits are reported (Schultz & Luthe 1969). Practitioners of ART also often claim an increase in their awareness of themselves and their reactions to their surroundings (Schultz & Luthe 1969; Lindeman 1974; Rosa 1976). A number of specific benefits have also been reported in the research literature. For instance, asthmatic attacks, insomnia and tension headaches occur less often (Wittkower & Warnes 1977; Rosa 1976). Also ART patients diagnosed as suffering from angina pectoris reported fewer myocardial infarctions when compared with patients relying on medication alone. Other studies suggest ART practitioners become less depressed and anxious. Sleep patterns may also improve and may be accompanied by an increase in alertness during waking hours (Luthe & Blumberger 1977; Lindeman 1974).

Clearly, ART, like other stress control techniques, is not a panacea for all stress in the health professions. For instance, it may not work effectively with practitioners who cannot make the mind-body link up with the verbal formulas of autogenic regulation training. Additionally, those people who are repeatedly exposed to stress-inducing situations may find it difficult to maintain their psychobiological homeostasis.

A 'saturation effect' may develop which has a major disrupting influence on the psychological functioning of the individual. When this is excessive, psychiatric illness may appear. Autogenic regulation training should not be used in these cases unless in close consultation with a clinical psychologist, qualified nurse or psychiatrist. However standard ART as it is set down here is an appropriate and efficacious method to practise with the softer psychological signs of stress such as anxiety, anger and mild depression. Insomnia, headaches, backache, bronchial asthma, writer's cramp, and other somatic complaints all show considerable improvement during and after autogenic regulation training (Schultz & Luthe 1969; Luthe & Blumberger 1977).

Perhaps the strongest reason for adopting ART is to use it as a method for preventing, or at least reducing, the threatening impact of demands in the individual's environment. From this point of view, autogenic regulation training seems to be a useful method which can be enlisted by professionals working in the field of health care — for themselves and for their patients.

STRESS-INNOCULATION TRAINING (SIT)

A fifth method of stress control involves adopting a comprehensive set of coping skills to deal with a wide range of stress-inducing situations; this approach has been developed by Donald Meichenbaum (1979). It is popularly termed *stress-innoculation training* (SIT). These coping skills involve you learning to modify your inner 'private dialogue'. The private dialogue that individuals have with themselves; what they say to themselves about situations; what they believe about the effects these may have on them and the memories of what threatens them and how they cope, influences whether or not they will experience some form of stress. The cognitive interpretation of each person influences his or her physical, mental, behavioural and emotional reaction to situations, and the feelings about the physiological activity in the body (Beck 1972, 1976).

For instance, a nurse may say to herself 'dying children makes my adrenalin flow and I feel anxious at not being able to help. In fact, I feel helpless.' (See, e.g., Senior Nurse Protocols, pp. 5–8). Adopting SIT procedures, the nurse can learn to alter her private dialogue for these types of situation and others. Different stages of SIT show how changing the labels and thoughts about threatening situations (e.g., as in nursing and medicine) can alter individual emotional reactions. Stress-innoculation training procedures can also be self-administered and, therefore, considerably reduce dependency on professional therapists.

The procedure for SIT usually involves four phases:

1 Educational
2 Behaviour rehearsal
3 Application
4 Self-reinforcement (on p. 108)

PREPARATION

Phase One — Education

During the education phase, the 'causes' of stress are explained by the counsellor in terms that you can understand rather than scientific concepts. In simple terms, the theory is conveyed to you in the following way:

1 We all interpret what goes on in our surroundings. It is these interpretations (or appraisals) which give rise to different sensations in our bodies.

2 When we get physiological sensations in our bodies, we try to make sense of them, in doing so we label our sensations to describe our states and moods, and general health.

3 It is these labels which give rise to whether or not we 'say' we are 'anxious, depressed, angry, elated, bored, calm, cool, or collected'.

Although this theory has been subjected to criticism (Meichenbaum 1979), it is still useful to conceptualize directly how stress arises, and by implication, how it can be controlled, and overcome. Just as we learn to label our sensations which then give rise to our experience of emotion, it is explained to the student that relabelling the environment, sensations, and how we think about them, can also change the emotions we experience. In turn, this relabelling and the change of the inner private dialogue we have should influence our physiological levels of arousal. One consequence of this *relabelling* of the environment, sensations, in relation to different levels of physiological activity is a reduction in reported stress reactions. After the education phase, you then rehearse the ideas learned in the education phase.

Phase Two — Behaviour Rehearsal

During behaviour rehearsal, you carry out the process of interpreting and relabelling the appraisals and different sensations you have identified as threatening. In clearly set out instructions, you practise 'talking to yourself' in different ways about situations which previously threatened you to the extent that they caused psychological and physical discomfort (Meichenbaum 1979). This application of 'coping self-talk' (Zastrow 1979) often achieves three goals. First, it changes the perception (primary appraisal) of the situation — usually resulting in a reduction in its threatening significance. Second, it allows you to take a less stressful view of the sensations experienced in your own body (secondary appraisal). Third, when these sensations are relabelled, they will usually result in your reporting dramatic reductions in experienced stress (re-appraisal). The essence of how physiological arousal is mediated by the way an individual labels his experience has been lucidly described by Meichenbaum (1979) and amounts to cognitive mediation of experience.

From this basis, a full programme of stress-innoculation instructions has been developed and tested with efficacious results (Meichenbaum 1979). The schedule of training permits you to move from the condition of learned helplessness (see, e.g., Seligman 1975; Abramson et al. 1978; Garber & Seligman 1980; Meichenbaum 1979) to one of acquired learned resourcefulness, renewed competence and progressive management of stress. The practitioners of stress-innoculation training develop more comprehensive appraisals and effective coping skills to increase the control of their own levels of stress. The education and behaviour rehearsal phases of SIT permit you to:

1 prepare for a threat that induces threat
2 confront and deal with stress-inducing threats
3 cope with feelings of inadequacy or being overwhelmed
4 achieve self-reinforcing statements which lead to personal control over stress

Phase Three — Application Practice

An example of a stress-innoculation training format which I have found useful shows how these stages can be utilised for the practice of personal control over stress. The format is:

Phase One — preparation

What do I have to do to cope effectively?
A coping plan will deal with it.
I am going to think out what has to be done.
Create positive statements and views of the demands.
Keep logical and rational, that's the way.
The stress and the worry don't help so forget about them.
If I'm anxious that is a sign of energy I can use for coping.

Phase Two — rehearsal

Keep it in your mind this is a challenge, you can cope with it.
Remember just take things one step at a time.
Keep cool and think it through.
Concentrate on what I'm doing. I've got the idea.
Stress is just a signal for coping. I was expecting this.
Keep in tune with the feelings, they help me to get coping.
I can use the tension, it gives me energy for coping.
It's 'good' to feel the tension, I can use it to control my stress
level.
My breathing is regular, calm and rhythmical.
This is the way to cope, keep it up.

Phase Three — application practice

Here come the demands. Get ready to apply my coping plan.
I am keeping focussed on my coping plan and putting it into
practice.
Any stress that comes. Just let it pass. I can note how pronounced it may be. But that is helpful. I know just what I
have to deal with.
I am managing well. The stress is under control.
I can carry on with my coping plan if I want too, or just do
enough to keep the demands manageable.
More preparation, rehearsal and practice will help me to
cope even more effectively with the demands of caring.

Phase Four — self reinforcement statements

I did do well. I must tell my colleagues how effective coping can be.

Maybe I even surprised myself.

I can use my stress more productively now.

I know now when I control my thoughts and act accordingly, I cope effectively. Looking at stress like this, I *can* be more competent.

And I know it will get better using this approach. I can also learn from any mistakes.

I have made tremendous progress. I *have* learned important new skills for coping.

Using a stress-innoculation training format of this kind also allows you to estimate how much threat you are under and how well you are coping. This can be done in a fairly detailed way. For instance, you can estimate how much difficulty you have with different situations, and the feelings and thoughts they engender. You may also get a clear idea of how well you cope with stress and the effect this has on yourself and demanding situations. Finally, you should be able to assess if your methods of coping are ones which promote control over threatening events and experienced stress.

A useful way of applying the SIT format is to measure your present reaction to threat, confrontation, feelings of being over-whelmed, and your kind of self-statements, before carrying out any stress-control programme. This is a principle which can be applied to the preceding methods of stress control. Doing this achieves at least two goals important for any stress-control assessment and training. First, it will give you 'a stress-control profile'. The profile would show both areas where you are doing well, and where you need help to establish or re-establish control over stress. Not all areas of the stress-control profile require a comprehensive scheme of stress-innoculation training. For example, a nurse may effectively prepare to meet a threat — such as being reprimanded by a superior in front of patients. She may also cope with feelings of embarrassment or anger, by being calm and polite without being servile (Allen 1980).

However, on the SIT assessment she may reveal being dissatisfied with the way she confronted such a situation. It is also possible she never congratulated herself on the dignified way in which she coped with the encounter. In such an instance, insufficient self-reinforcing statements leading to personal control would be evident. This example of a baseline assessment prior to SIT highlights a second goal. The SIT profile informs the nurse and therapist which parts of the nurse's reactions to the situation have to be changed. In this case, the nurse could be taught to confront 'being shown up in front of patients' by:

1   ignoring the incident
2   asking to discuss the matter in private
3   suggesting it should be written down and discussed at a later date when she is not so busy, or
4   relabelling her present view of how she confronted the incident

Relabelling could involve her saying to herself, 'this is below my dignity', 'I am handling this the right way, I am calm and in control', 'this is a matter which is of no importance to me' and other self-talk which would neutralize the threatening significance of the experienced situation. The activation of relabelling would also be followed by self-reinforcing statements such as, 'I didn't panic', 'staying cool was the right thing to do', 'I'm glad I reacted the way I did', 'I have control of the situation and myself', etc. These are examples of self-statements which promote control over potentially stressful threatening demands in the health professions. Once these have been established, the goal-efficacy of the programme can be evaluated.

Phase Four — Self-reinforcement Statements

Notice how particular attention is given to the reinforcing self-statements that support the control over stress. This helps to promote and maintain effecting coping.

EVALUATION

In its simplest form, evaluation can be done by going through each stage of the SIT programme. The typical sequence involves checking once again reactions to each stage of SIT training. In the preceding example, we would check that the nurse still felt prepared to deal with the threat and cope with her feelings. But we would expect her to use a different style of confrontation and self-reinforcing statements leading to an increase in personal control. This change in style and relabelling would show up in the nurse's response to the stages outlined in the SIT programme. Where these therapeutic changes were noted, we should find a corresponding decrease in the forms of reported stress. The nurse's self-reports are now likely to indicate a state of satisfactory well-being. The nurse will have achieved a desirable state of control and psychobiological homeostasis as a consequence of employing SIT procedures.

Stress-innoculation training would, therefore, seem to have an important part to play in the health professions. Its main contribution would be in helping caregiving professionals to maximize their control over threat, and enhancing their coping skills to combat disabling forms of stress such as acute anxiety, reactive depression and anger. Its main appeal lies in the practitioner being able to adopt a varied range of appraisal and coping skills within and across different threatening situations. Initially, for the most part SIT, like the other methods of stress control detailed in this chapter, can be self-administered after a short period of supervised practice.

PRACTICAL CONSIDERATIONS AND SPECULATIONS FOR FUTURE STRESS CONTROL

The stress-control and self-regulation coping strategies covered in this chapter present a number of realistic options open to health professionals who wish to practise stress control for themselves and their patients. Training in stress-control techniques could also be adopted by schools and colleges of nursing, and medical schools, and incorporated into their education curricula. Nursing management, district and regional health authorities should also support and research the efficacy of stress control on patient and health and caregiving effectiveness.

Data have been collated which show a significant relationship between nurse sickness records and autogenic regulation training (Bailey 1984a). The experimental or autogenic regulation training group showed considerably less recorded sickness than a control group of nurse students. Thus there is a further potential benefit. Nursing in general may also become more cost effective from a management-administrative perspective by the practice of stress-control methods. We can speculate further still and suggest that doctors, nurse tutors and qualified ward management nurses would also benefit from introducing and using some of the techniques discussed in this chapter to avoid or reduce already disabling levels of stress. However, these areas should be properly researched for their association with other financial and health care variables rather than being introduced uncritically into medical practice, nursing and health care systems. At present though, we can have considerable clinical confidence in offering a range of stress-control techniques for use by a wide range of health professionals which at least provides a coherent means of coping with threat or stress. The techniques I have considered here can be self-administered after an initial period of training by appropriately qualified nurses, therapists, doctors or clinical psychologists.

Stress control techniques can be used to prepare nurses and other allied health professionals for dealing with predictable threatening aspects of their environment. Unexpected or unpredictable sources of threat, common to nurses (HMSO 1972), may also be 'defused' through the regular practice of stress-control techniques. Other benefits might also stem from the very knowledge that the health professions involved have the means to control their levels of stress — even though they do not put them into practice. Just knowing that they can exert some control over disturbing internal or external threats such as pain or anxiety is in itself enough to limit the impact of otherwise stress-producing events in life (Garber & Seligman 1980; Pervin 1963; Bailey 1984a; Glass & Singer 1972).

Controlling stress should also 'immunize' the health professions against helplessness (Seligman 1975; Abramsom *et al.* 1978; Garber & Seligman 1980). In this respect, acquiring stress-control techniques and practising them are not to be confused as the same thing. Although they both seem to be connected with achieving control over stress-inducing threats in the context of delivering health care systems. We can conclude therefore that the availability of stress-control techniques may serve a significant function in maintaining and promoting human health amongst nurses and allied health professionals.

STRESS-CONTROL METHODS — AN OVERVIEW

Health professionals have to face many demands which threaten them to the extent that they can experience different forms of stress. The stress experienced may be acute and psychophysiological, emotional or physical in its manifestations.

Five methods of stress control were considered in detail and practice protocols outlined. These were:

1 Progressive relaxation (PR)
2 Relaxation with desensitization (SD)
3 Transcendental meditation (TM)
4 Autogenic regulation training (ART)
5 Stress-innoculation training (SIT)

These methods of stress control are proposed as being useful approaches to gaining control over stress.

Health professionals should be able to practise them on their own after a training period of supervision by a competent therapist or clinical psychologist suitably qualified in the principles and practice of stress control methods.

CHAPTER FIVE

BREATHING —
THE BRIDGE TO STRESS CONTROL

All of the approaches to stress control have one thing in common — breathing. We all breathe in regular, rhythmical and regular or irregular episodic rhythms. Breathing is constant, but not necessarily consistent. In fact our breathing alters with our 'state of mind'.

STRESS AND BREATH

Short gasping breaths are often associated with panic and anxiety (Johnston 1983; Volin 1980). And irregular exhalations such as sighs are clinically connected with depression (Bailey 1984b). Changes in breathing are also often linked to changes in heart rate. So for instance, when the heart rate speeds up (*tachycardia*), breathing may become irregular, heavy and shallow. Likewise, if the heart rate slows down (*bradycardia*), breathing may become deep with long intervals between each breath. We can see then how breathing should be of central concern to us, not only in the stress control procedures I exemplified earlier but in our everyday lives.

Clearly, breathing is involved (at least indirectly) in everything we do in our provision of care to client and patient groups. Health professionals such as nurses, doctors, social workers, remedial therapists and radiographers cannot deny this fact. It is a truism. There is clear evidence that the way we breathe influences how we feel, and how we feel influences how we breathe. Nurses and their colleagues in allied health professions who are exposed to demanding environments need to be able to realize how breathing *correctly* can produce feelings and states

112

of mind which combat stress. Correct breathing is the bridge to stress control, and composed professional alertness (Bailey 1984b, Ramachakara 1974).

CORRECT BREATHING

Breathing Awareness

Breathing awareness is the first step we should take in our efforts to attain correct breathing. Just stop doing what you are doing for a few moments and focus your attention onto your breathing. Take note of how you are breathing.

Are you consciously making an effort to breathe in and out?

Are the exhalations comfortable and natural or does a feeling of tightness surround your diaphragm, chest, abdomen, and lungs?

Are your inhalations and exhalations equal in length and duration, or are they unbalanced?

In carrying out this breathing awareness activity you can begin to identify if you are breathing correctly. One of the signs that your breathing is not in a natural rhythm is if the breathing cycles are in any way hurried or fast and irregular.

Slow and Regular

Correct breathing is slow and regular. To get the feel of the effects of slow and regular breathing carry out this simple exercise.

Gradually, expel all the air out of your lungs: Do this as slowly as possible without it being painful in any way.

Then, let the inhalation take place spontaneously. You will find this happens naturally. Just let it happen.

By doing this breathing exercise you can begin to correct some of the errors of breathing you discovered in your breathing awareness activity. Repeat the gradual exhalation and spontaneous inhalation up to 10 repetitions until you begin to feel the effects of the exercise.

Nasal Breathing

Many of us breathe through our mouths although we are often not aware of it. You may have found that you were breathing orally when you conducted the breathing awareness exercise. If you breathe orally this is not correct breathing. Breathing orally interrupts the natural functions of the breath. These are not just to replenish the organism with sufficient supplies of oxygen. Among the main functions of breathing, regulating the psycho-physiological processes of the individual is of central importance. Another function of correct breathing is its inherent potential for reducing stress (Bailey 1984b; Volin 1980). Consequently correct breathing helps to promote general health and feelings of psychological well-being (Bailey 1984a; von Lysebeth 1983). This is done by the use of breathing to facilitate healing and a balance between the interfused systems of body-mind-feelings, behaviour or actions and spiritual wellness (Schultz & Luthe 1959; Bailey 1984b; von Lysebeth 1983; Watts 1982, 1983).

Nasal breathing is more natural. But more important, by breathing correctly through the nostrils control over stress can be achieved more rapidly, and competent composure attained (Bailey 1984b; Watts 1982; Suzuki 1982). Nurses and those in other health caring professions should benefit from correcting their breathing to nasal breathing. I regard this as an essential preparation for effective stress control and other breathing exercises (Bailey 1984b; Johnston 1983; Volin 1980).

Natural and Rhythmical

By now you may have noticed that correct breathing has a natural rhythm of its own. This does not mean that any two people breathe exactly the same or should breathe in the same pattern of inhalations and exhalations. Rather, it points to the common yet individual nature of breathing. The common features are the inhalations and exhalations. They form a pattern. They constitute the cycles of breath which rhythmically occur when we are breathing in a natural manner.

The individual profile of breathing patterns and rhythms formed by the breathing cycles are variable. So, when you are correcting your breathing to control stress, or better still to prevent certain stress such as feeling anxious, don't try to copy anyone else's inhalations and exhalations to discover *your* natural rhythm of breathing. This is imitation and usually meets with undesirable results such as tightness and feeling unnatural. All that is often achieved is learning to breathe like somebody else. What is required is to breathe as yourself. This means *allowing* your own natural rhythm of breathing to take place. The exercises outlined later in this chapter should help to facilitate these beneficial effects.

A clue to the changing over from incorrect to correct breathing can, however, be observed:

First, estimate the length and form of the inhalations and exhalations and how you feel.

Then, carry out slow and regular breathing and breathe nasally for about 5 minutes.

Allow your breath to 'take over'. But follow it by being aware of what is happening to your inhalation and exhalation patterns and the feelings you have.

Note these down and compare them with your initial observations of your breathing patterns. When you have begun to breathe correctly you should simply be able to apply and observe your breathing unobtrusively and let its natural rhythm serve your professional purposes such as the need to be 'calm, cool and collected' or 'cogent, competent and in command' of demanding circumstances (Bailey 1984a, 1984b; Bailey and Clarke in preparation). In my view, nurses and other health professionals should bring correct breathing into operation whenever 1) stress is anticipated or 2) being currently experienced. Clearly, deviations from correct breathing are early warning signs of stress. Incorrect breathing may also be connected with many of the symptoms indicative of burn-out in the helping professions (Bailey 1984b).

PREPARATION AND PRACTICE

Correct breathing should help you to prepare yourself for the practice of breathing as a natural method of stress control. Correct breathing can also be used in conjunction with the stress control procedures discussed in the last chapter. By adopting correct breathing with the help of specific breathing exercises you can obtain a number of personal benefits. When correct breathing is present you will breathe without strain or effort. Breathing will begin to become diaphragmmatic breathing, and the breathing impulse will emanate from the diaphragm and the abdomen, moving upwards to fill the chest and rib areas of the body.

Correct breathing also enables you to gain personal control over stress and also promote calming and alertness (Petersen 1979). All are necessary and important attributes of the competent health professional.

Sensing the Breath

Preparation also means getting used to the sensations of breathing. You should be able to do this by carrying out the breathing awareness activity exercise, and developing nasal and rhythmical breathing. These are all essential elements in preparation for correct breathing. To begin with being aware of your breathing and the exercises which facilitate correct breathing will probably seem unnatural. This is to be expected. For just like learning a new skill so it is with correct breathing. We know how to breathe, or at least we have established a habit of breathing in a particular way. Your task is to find out if you are breathing in such a way that is unnatural, stressful or adds to any stressful experiences you may have had. Correct breathing is natural, stress-free, and indeed has beneficial effects which aid human functioning and professional effectiveness (Bailey 1984b; Volin 1980).

Stillness and Starting Off

A useful way to start off developing correct breathing is simply to observe, or *watch*, the stillness generated through breathing. By 'watching your breath', a stillness begins to be experienced. This is often associated with feelings of calmness and restfulness. Accompanying these feelings will often be a sense of growing resourcefulness, greater awareness and restful alertness (Bailey 1984b; Petersen 1979; Volin 1980; Ramachakara 1974; Watts 1983). You can start to contact this stillness by focussing your awareness on your breathing and completing this exercise.

Breathe out, and as you do count slowly but regularly and rhythmically from 1 through to 10. When you get to 10 begin to inhale for a count of 10.

Now repeat the exhalation procedure and inhalation procedure as one: breathing out for a count of 10 then breathing in for a count of 10.

Continue to repeat this stilling exercise for at least 20 cycles of 10 exhalations and inhalations.

Then note any effects you have experienced such as coolness in the nostrils and head, calming, stillness, clarity of thought, and composure. You may also want to note down any physical effects as well; for instance slowing of the heartbeat and length of inhalations and exhalations. Modulating of body temperature may also happen as you begin to produce the effects associated with this stilling exercise. Starting off in this way helps to combine the stillness exercise with rhythmical breathing, and awareness of the breath.

A good guide to the stilling exercise can also be seen when inhalations and exhalations are of equal length. So that

Inhalation = Exhalation.

This is a helpful practical approach to stress control. It also makes it possible for health professionals, indeed all caregivers, to prepare themselves for predictably difficult periods of work.

Equally important, when stress often occurs as a result of unpredictable and demanding circumstances, the stilling technique may be adopted to help individuals 'maintain a composed competence and gather themselves' before proceeding to deal with the demands being made upon them. Do not force any of the breaths you take and remember to allow the rhythm of breathing to take its own course, once it starts to respond to the exercise.

These breathing exercises are a bridge to stress control and correct breathing. The techniques outlined in this chapter are meant to *facilitate* (but not replace) and enhance correct and natural breathing cycles.

Cutting Down on Stress by Slowing-up the Breath

One of the best ways to cut down on stress is by decreasing the number of breaths we take between inhalations and exhalations. This is something which requires a little concentration at first, for it is not generally a natural process. It will become easier as you practise 'slowing' of the breath, which is particularly effective in reducing a state of panic or manic behaviour in people. Prolonged exhalations in particular produce stilling effects and help the individual to recover control over his or her emotions. This approach to stress control also helps to balance your mind, body and concentration. It should be of benefit to those in the health professions who are often expected to deal with urgent and unpredictable demands made by patients and colleagues (HMSO 1972).

Prolonged exhalation is one of the main ways to reduce the number of breaths. This helps to achieve stilling and generally calming effects.

You should exhale very slowly and so gently that the flow of air would not disturb a feather attached to the tip of your nose.

Again, no exhalation efforts should involve conscious effort or physical pain. If you experience pain, then the breath is being forced through the nostrils. Pain is a sign that you are trying too hard to produce the stilling and composing effects brought about by this exercise. The result is an increase of tension, the opposite of the beneficial effects usually produced by slowing the breath. In other words by slowing the breath you control the stress and release tension.

Inhalations

Inhalations should be allowed to occur as a 'spontaneous surge' at the end of each exhalation. This surge is part of the spontaneous breathing reflex. But we can increase its responsiveness by slowing the breath. Doing this you will also begin to increase your control over the breathing reflex. Yet, at the same time you begin you will find the breathing reflex strengthening. All of these signs indicate you are carrying out the exercise correctly. They help you to get the maximum benefit out of slowing the breath as a breathing exercise. Slowing the breathing helps to harness the natural breathing reflex and cut down on unwanted stress. You should find quick relief from practising this exercise. The more practised you become the longer lasting will be the beneficial effects of slowing the breath. But remember during inhalations using this breathing procedure, the air is automatically sucked into the lungs. Let this happen. Make no effort to control the amount of oxygen you inhale and avoid trying to make the inhalation last the same amount of time as the exhalation. Remember, this exercise is not aimed at balancing the breath; its main intention is to effect stilling and calming in the individual.

Once this is achieved, you and your patients who practise stilling through prolonged exhalation and spontaneous inhalations may proceed to regular and balanced breathing. Prolonging exhalation helps to focus the individual on *controlling* stress through the modulation of the breath. Inhalation provides the 'fuel' from which this control can and does emerge. Carrying out this exercise also helps the breathing impulse to emanate from the diaphragm and not the thorax. A point which should not be overlooked in allowing the breath to follow its natural response (Bailey 1984c; Watts 1983; Suzuki 1982).

'Following the Breath'

By systematically carrying out these breathing procedures you will find that your breath soon becomes regulated and without strain. Remember that the air should be taken in and expelled through the nose. This is one of the basic rules of breath control. Oral breathing seems to be a barrier to quietening the mind and easing the emotions.

You will know that you are following your breath when you:

1   Begin to sense the air travelling in, through, and out of your nostrils.

2   Sense a rhythm or natural cycle of inhalations and exhalations developing.

3   Experience growing control over your breathing processes.

4   Sense silencing, calming and stilling effects growing out of your breathing cycles.

5   Find you are composed, relaxed and in a state of restful alertness.

6   Discover also other breathing related effects such as coolness, clarity of thought and personal well-being.

SPECIFIC BREATHING SKILLS

The way in which we have considered breathing so far helps to point out the essential elements of breathing in stress control. Breathing correctly and naturally and having control of the breath can all act as bridges to stress control. Put in its simplest terms breathing as well as being a sign of stress can also be enlisted by the individual as a form of effective coping. Correct breathing can help health professionals cope with stress arising out of caring for others (Bailey 1984b). The general elements of breath control can also be seen in exercises aimed at establishing specific breathing skills in the practitioner. One of these is called *watching the breath* (Johnston 1983; Volin 1980).

'Watching the Breath'

Watching the breath means just what it says. The practitioner of this exercise literally observes what is happening to the breath as he or she carries out the exercise. This is sometimes more difficult to achieve than you think at first. Allowing ourselves to breathe and at the same time guiding the breath into a particular way of breathing takes practice and time. The time should be spent

avoiding interfering with the way the breath begins to respond to a particular breathing procedure and

making certain the procedure is adhered to for inhalations and exhalations.

Paradoxically, by both allowing the breath to take its own course and yet at the same time disciplining it to a procedure, a process of different breathing emerges. This can be practised either for competence, calming or restful alertness training (Volin 1980). Health professionals should find practising watching the breath useful for themselves and their patients.

PROCEDURE FOR 'WATCHING THE BREATH' EXERCISE

Step One — Releasing the Breath

Begin by gradually and completely releasing your breath. Remember to do this through your nostrils. Feel the air being compressed out of your body. The effect experienced should be something like a bellows being deflated. Allow it to come out from the diaphragm up into the thorax and down the nasal canal. Continue to exhale until you have expelled as much air as possible without incurring discomfort.

Step Two — Capturing the Breath

Now fresh air is 'captured' by a spontaneous inward breath. The term *captured* is used to convey the idea that you should suddenly and reflexively inhale immediately after the release of breath. Just let it happen. Do not make any active or conscious efforts to draw in air during this phase of the breathing cycle. This form of inhalation has been called 'gasping at air' (Watts 1983) and does not help to produce calming or alerting states. In fact, as we have seen already this is incorrect breathing and may also lead to, or be associated with, stress states such as anxiety helplessness and depression (Speilberger 1972; Seligman 1975).

Step Three — Repeating the Cycles

The process of exhalation and inhalation, of releasing and capturing the breath, constitutes a complete cycle in watching the breath. These should repeated for 1-, 5-, 10-. or 15-minute sessions.

To begin with you may be aware of the steps you are taking to establish the cycle of breath, but this usually diminishes after practice. Sometimes the rhythm can be established very quickly. This is more likely to happen if some time is set aside for regular practice in breathing exercises.

The cycles of breath should be repeated so that you begin to experience a sense of ebbing and flowing of the breath. In addition, sensations of lightness and heaviness alternating with each breath can be observed. Other signs may be present such as heaviness, warmth and feeling you are glowing. These are all signs that the rhythm of the cycle is being established.

Keep practising this exercise until you can notice your breathing following a renewed natural path of inhalation and exhalation rhythms.

BREATH CONTROL AS A MEANS OF STRESS CONTROL

Before achieving new and responsive natural rhythms in the cycles of breathing, we have seen how some control must first be exerted over the breathing habits of the individual. You may recall how at sometime in your career you have either told or been told to 'control yourself' or 'pull yourself together' and 'control yourself and calm down'. Earlier we saw how burn-out in caregivers is often associated with the feeling of losing control of their emotions or having little control over events in their professional environment. This is typically observed in symptoms such as loss of motivation, depression, feelings of helplessness and disinterest in work (Moores & Grant 1977; Oswin 1978; Seligman 1975). Perhaps of great concern is the frequent low self-esteem found amongst health professionals who perceive they have hardly any control over the occupations which they carry out (Bailey 1982b; Claus & Bailey 1980; Marshall 1980; Moores & Grant 1977; Oswin 1978). Controlling the breath is one effective way to control stress. Especially under the often 'unpredictable demands' and sometimes catastrophic circumstances the helping professions have to cope with (Bailey 1981, 1982b, 1983a; HMSO 1972; Murray 1976).

Exercising Breath Control to Avoid or Combat Stress

You can develop breath control first of all by concentrating on the breath itself. This is similar to the awareness of breath exercise. But the effects of breath control to overcome or avoid stress can be enhanced further by employing the following techniques:

BASIC TRAINING IN BREATH CONTROL

Step One — Finding a Space

Find a space or quiet corner. When you have done this start to concentrate and focus on your breathing. You can sit or lie down for this exercise. But it can also be carried out in demanding situations such as those associated with ICU nursing, mental handicap nursing, general medical practice, rehabilitation patients, and the problems of helping patients with acute or chronic illnesses (Moos 1979). These are often reported as causes of stress in caring (Bailey 1983b).

Step Two — the Breathing Cycle

Focus on your inhalations and exhalations. Observe the cycles of the breath. Feel the air filling and being discharged from your nostrils, thorax, lungs, and abdomen. Note any cool sensations during inhalations and composing warming tranquil effects during the outward breath. Allow the natural cycle of inhalations and exhalations to develop until your breathing becomes symmetrical and regulated.

Step Three — Regulated Breathing — Consolidating Stress Control

As you continue to regulate your breathing allow the sense of calmness, alertness and ready composure to spread throughout your body. Allow this to happen and imagine it to radiate through you like healing rays and observe how regulated your breathing becomes. A sense of balance and control should develop as your breathing cycle is consolidated. You can get some idea of breathing becoming regulated and consolidated when this 'new' breathing pattern begins to occur without effort. Continue to practise until you can produce the balanced breath and regulated control over inhalations and exhalations. You should find this exercise in breath control helpful as a preventive or remedial procedure for managing stress.

'Take a Deep Breath and Count to Ten'

How many times have we found ourselves in the situation where someone has come to us bursting with anger or in an anxious panic? Do we ask them to sit down? Offer them some water to drink? Or, as I have sometimes found, ask them to take a deep breath and count to ten? Let's examine this a little further.

First, why ask anyone to take a deep breath and then count to ten? In my view this is a simple 'first aid' way to help the person control his or her stress level. Even though this is a temporary form of psychological first-aid, it allows people 'a breathing space'. A space in which they can start to manage their stress problem. I have found a variation of taking a deep breath and counting to ten useful for those health professionals who have to deal with upsetting emergencies and anger-inducing conflicts at work. I call this technique *spacing the breath*.

'Spacing the Breath'

Spacing the breath consists of deliberately creating spaces or intervals during and between each breath (Bailey 1984b). It is not as complicated as it sounds. The intervals which space out the breath are regulated by counting or some other spacing regulator such as a metronome. I have found the counting method preferable for two reasons: First, we seldom have metronomes available to us. Second, the way in which I use counting in the procedure, encourages you to develop control over stress by pairing your breathing with internal counting. In other words, the counting method is silently repeated to oneself. The prime benefit from this I believe is that the internal counting guides the breath, so that the spacing of the breath is governed by the *rate* of counting.

Another important factor in spacing the breath is the *interval* between each number as you repeat them to yourself. Intervals between counting are not the same thing as the rate of counting. For example, it is possible to space the breath to a count of 10 for inhalation, for 5 holding the breath, and 10 for exhalations. Other combinations of inhalation, holding and exhalations can be made and should be adapted for each person's preference. Here, I am merely illustrating one way in which rate of counting can be used in spacing the breath.

For intervals, supposing we take the schedule of counting 10 inhalations, 5 for holding the breath and 10 again for exhalations and repeated this cycle of breathing. Intervals of breath concern the *time* between each count. In the example we could have intervals of 1 second or say 2 seconds between each count. Putting this together we develop a complete procedure for spacing the breath. We can say the rate of breath is a count of 10 for inhalation, 5 for holding and 10 for exhalations. The interval between each count should be 1 second. You can then space the breath by adopting the following procedure:

PROCEDURE FOR 'SPACING THE BREATH' EXERCISE

Step One — Beginning

Begin by taking note of your usual breathing pattern. Record the length and frequency of your inhalations and exhalations. Also make a note of any psychological effects such as tension, aggravation or anxiousness. Physical sensations such as pain, cramps or fatigue should be written down or kept on a cassette or computer file. These can be referred to subsequently to compare possible relationships between breathing and symptoms of stress.

Step Two — Inward Breath

After carrying out step one and establishing a baseline, move on to step two. Here you should focus on nasal inhaling and control your breath using the counting method. In this step, as suggested you count from 1 through to 10 inhaling with a pause of about 1 second between counts. So your inward breath during step two should be nasal inhale, 1, pause, 2, pause, 3, pause, 4, pause, and so on until you reach the point of inhalation where you have reached the tenth point of the inhalation. At this point you will have moved into step three of spacing the breath.

Step Three — Holding

Hold your breath for the same counting strategy; but for a count of 5 with intermediate pauses each 1 second in length. So in this exercise you hold the breath and count 1, pause, 2, pause, 3, pause and so on again until you reach the fifth point of holding the breath. (Holding the breath is not a contest to see who can do it longest.) Step three is then naturally followed by step four, which is the outward breath.'

Step Four — Outward Breath

The final part of spacing the breath is applied during exhalation. Again the air should be passed down the nostrils. But in spacing the breath you should adhere to the count from 1 through to 10 with 1 second intervals as you carried out during the inward breath. Sometimes I have found practitioners become quite quickly relaxed during the outward breath. A sign which is obviously encouraging. But try *not* to abandon the counting method if you are also trying to achieve control over your breathing cycles.

As we have seen already, control comes first. When this is done you can give way to the spontaneous and refreshing natural breathing cycles. Occasionally, you may only want to gain quick relief, at the expense of longer-term control over your breathing. If this is the case you should still be able to complete steps one, two, three and four of spacing the breath more quickly by reducing the count, e.g., only count to 5 after each stage. In step four, the outward breath can also be released in a 'gush'. This allows a quick discharge of air through the nasal passages *and* thorax and abdomen. It usually brings feelings of comfort and relief (Bailey 1984b; Watts 1983).

Some people occasionally find that discharging the air through the mouth rapidly brings them feelings of tension reduction and calmness. In discharging the final step of spacing the breath through the mouth, you should make a sound similar to an extended P . . . . . . ah. Then continue with the cycle of breathing involving the inward breath, holding and counting, until you come to step four again where you can discharge the waste air through your mouth. Strictly speaking however, step four of spacing the breath should be a mirror image of the inward breath and therefore reflect the counting method for breath control. Continue spacing the breath for a predetermined 5, 10, 15, or even 20 minutes. Then allow your breathing to proceed completely spontaneously.

Checking Practice

Any stress control, or self-esteem enhancing exercise should be checked for its efficacy and practical consequences. Using breathing techniques as a bridge to stress control is no exception to this principle. Therefore it is generally helpful and informative to take baseline and repeated subsequent measures of different aspects of functioning prior to practising the techniques I have outlined in this chapter. Outcome measures should also be taken and comparisons made between pre-practice and post-practice effects. These effects can be quite general such as improvements in your overall state of health, well-being, energy level, alertness, and estimate of tensions relaxation level. (See Stress-check Schedules in Appendices for ways by which this can be carried out.) Specific measures may also monitor the relationships between breathing cycles and stress. Typical specific indices here are temperature, pulse, respiration, anxiety, depression, anger, time taken to complete tasks. Somatic monitoring is also important. Estimates of somatic functioning such as backache, headaches and tolerance for pain can be assessed for their intensity and degree of association with different patterns of breathing.

BREATHING — THE LINK BETWEEN THOUGHT, FEELINGS AND ACTION

Why all the fuss about breathing? There are a number of reasons why breathing cycles are central to stress management. First, breathing is linked to the way we think, and the way we think is related to our breathing. Put this into your own experience for a moment. Just imagine how difficult it is to experience panic or anxiety and have smooth and slow regulated natural rhythms of the breath. Similarly enjoying the composure of professional competence is not usually connected with the racing breath of fear and anger or the exhausting sighs of grief.

Though we like to separate them for convenience of analysis and problem-solving, breathing and thinking are interfused with each other (Suzuki 1982). In addition to this, breathing is also connected with the actions we take in our professional practice and as individuals. The same holds true for patients, their thoughts, breathing and essential feelings or actions. By actions, I mean the range of behaviours we engage in at any one time. For instance, lifting patients is a set of behaviours which constitute an action. Not only this, proper and efficient breathing is necessary for efficient lifting. Serious weightlifters know how concentrated use of the breath helps them in lifting.

Lifting is not the only example of breathing influencing behaviour. Take the complicated action of writing. A certain amount of fine musculature control and psychological composure is necessary before the complex graphics we recognize as writing can take place. Breathing patterns which induce restlessness or states of general agitation are conducive to neither composed writing nor well-being.

A further point about breathing, thoughts, feelings and actions is simply that they do not exist independently of each other. There is more than this though. I am also suggesting that they influence each other continuously. So many possible combinations exist between breathing, thoughts, feelings and actions. Reciprocal influences therefore exist which are immensely important for our understanding of stress and coping.

All this makes what was originally quite simple, now dauntingly complex. Yet, for anyone concerned with the field of coping with stress in caring, it provides a useful conceptual framework. It is useful in at least three ways. First, it highlights how breathing can be related to thoughts, feelings and actions. Second, it provides one way in which separate aspects of stress and coping can be identified and assessed. Third, and particularly important, it allows us to evaluate the role breathing practices, thoughts, feelings and actions have separately or together in reducing or increasing stress. In other words we have a strategy to help us investigate the question, how well are the health professionals coping with stress. This approach is consistent with the framework for understanding stress and coping discussed earlier (see Chapter 2). The transactional links between breathing, thoughts, feelings, and actions can also be graphically presented (see Figure 7).

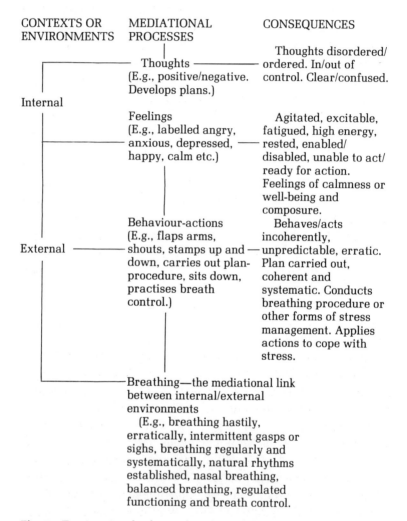

CONTEXTS OR   MEDIATIONAL   CONSEQUENCES
ENVIRONMENTS   PROCESSES

Thoughts
(E.g., positive/negative. Develops plans.)

Internal

Thoughts disordered/ ordered. In/out of control. Clear/confused.

Feelings
(E.g., labelled angry, anxious, depressed, happy, calm etc.)

Agitated, excitable, fatigued, high energy, rested, enabled/ disabled, unable to act/ ready for action. Feelings of calmness or well-being and composure.

Behaviour-actions
(E.g., flaps arms, shouts, stamps up and down, carries out plan-procedure, sits down, practises breath control.)

External

Behaves/acts incoherently, unpredictable, erratic. Plan carried out, coherent and systematic. Conducts breathing procedure or other forms of stress management. Applies actions to cope with stress.

Breathing—the mediational link between internal/external environments
(E.g., breathing hastily, erratically, intermittent gasps or sighs, breathing regularly and systematically, natural rhythms established, nasal breathing, balanced breathing, regulated functioning and breath control.

Fig. 7 Transactional relationships between breathing, thoughts, feelings, and behaviour-actions model.

Familiarity with the Transactional Relationship Model

You should spend some time getting to know the relationships which exist in this transactional model. It is an analogue or theoretical map of how stress and coping are related to breathing, our thoughts, feelings, behaviour-actions, and the environments or contexts in which they take place. But not only is it a theoretical map, it is also something you will be able to see is easily translated into practical, and practicable, terms. Here is a useful way of understanding and using it. First, notice how the transactional map of relationships all link up with each other. The network lines show the possible range of connections that can be made. These connections also suggest how the different relationships between contexts or environments, breathing and their consequences can be associated with thoughts and feelings. These relationships also involve internal or external environments. So for example a typical internal relationship exists between how we feel and our breathing. If we feel anxious our breathing may be shallow and irregular. Other examples are anger and relaxation. In the former breathing is likely to be deeper and breath holding may occur. The latter — feeling relaxed — is usually associated with regular rhythmical breathing. This model also shows the way in which different relationships can influence each other. Thoughts, feelings, breathing, and behaviour-actions are all inter-related and mutually influence each other in any given context.

Some further familiarity with the model in Figure 7 should make it possible for us to gain an even clearer idea of the complexities of stress and coping. I want to emphasize two points about it: the conceptual combinations of continuous influential relationships between breathing, thoughts, feelings, and behaviour-actions, and, equally relevant, how this conceptual framework can be applied in practice.

CONCEPTUAL COMBINATIONS FOR STRESS AND COPING

A number of conceptual combinations for stress and coping can be inferred from Figure 8. These can be related to the way you cope with the demands of caring. Additionally they may also be assessed for their utility value in coping with stress, and facilitating or inhibiting the management of stress. Categorizing these feasible functional relationships under type and some examples shows how these conceptual combinations for stress and coping and the transactional model can be understood and practised.

Breathing	Regular/Irregular Natural/Forced Symmetrical/Asymmetrical, spasmodic interval, rate. Context-related
Thoughts	Positive/Negative thinking Stress-alleviating/Stress inducing Realistic/Unrealistic Temporary/Persistent. Range, Context-related
Feelings	Positive effect (enhancing) Negative effect (limiting) Transitory/Persistent Range. Appropriate/Inappropriate Context-related
Behaviour-actions	Temporary/Persistent Short-term/Long-term Appropriate/Inappropriate Coping-effecting/ineffective Context-related

Fig. 8   Categories of relationships model.

Functional and Dysfunctional Relationships

All these categories can be either functional or dysfunctional to the individual. Functional relationships also have many shared properties such as the context where they take place, how long they last and whether they are appropriate or coping effective in managing stress. From your own viewpoint, most of the contexts for example are likely to be associated with work. Thoughts, feelings and behaviour-actions if appropriate are also going to be connected with occupational demands (Bailey 1983a). They are all inextricably connected and play an essential role coping with stress and the demands of caring. For instance, by adopting a rational approach to problem-solving, or by employing breath control procedures in situations associated with panic. These functional relationships are interdependent in practice. It is a truism of life that we are breathing, thinking, feeling, and carrying out courses of action all of the time. These are all part of continuing interconnected processes with each able to influence the other in functional or dysfunctional ways. Applying the model we have the example of health professionals who can conduct themselves in a particular way which also feeds back to them and in turn again maintains or alters their thoughts, feelings and behaviour and breathing. This can happen at any point in the continuing process of these functional relationships. So we can have:

Breathing	influencing	Thoughts, Feelings, Behaviour-actions
Thoughts	influencing	Breathing, Feelings, Behaviour-actions
Feelings	influencing	Breathing, Thoughts, Behaviour-actions
Behaviour-actions	influencing	Breathing, Thoughts, Feelings

All these act in tandem with each other and produce what we call experience. These experiences we then label as happy, angry, sad, competent, calm, confused, alert, confident, and so on. They can be applied to practical coping for health professionals. We have already seen how this can be done separately. But they can also be controlled and employed consciously in various combinations, engaged as attempts to facilitate effective coping. The results may of course be functional or dysfunctional in their outcomes.

Depending on the categories of relationships these can be utilized in two main ways. First, the helping health professionals may better understand stress and coping and how it influences them and their patients. Second, of equal importance, health professionals should be able to combine the categories and types of relationships to help them cope better. Coping by combining breathing with thinking is one example.

COMBINING BREATHING AND THINKING — AN EXAMPLE OF COMBINED COPING

It is sometimes helpful to combine autogenic regulation training with the natural rhythm of breathing. For instance, the practitioner can combine the categories of breathing and thinking to produce states of restful alertness. You can test this out for yourself. Take yourself through this exercise:

Establish autogenic relaxation by practising the standard autogenic exercises (see Chapter 4) and allowing the thoughts of warmth, heaviness, comfort, calmness, and peacefulness .to develop. Then experience these states and make a record of when they come about. Alongside this, begin to allow your breathing to become natural and rhythmical. Also let your breathing synchronize with the autogenic statements you are making to yourself. So that you have inhalations and exhalations matched with autogenic instructions such as 'I am cool, comfortable and calm'.

Other breathing-statement relationships can then be built onto and fused with these relaxation–natural breathing combinations. Here you can also effectively introduce the idea of being alert and resourceful and link this with your breathing. For instance, you might say to yourself 'I am cogent, competent and composed'. Accompany these thoughts with each inward and outward breathing cycle. In other words regulate your thinking with your breathing, and develop the two in synchrony with each other. You will then soon see how the functional relationships between breathing and thinking can be enlisted by you. These functional combinations provide an effective way of coping with stress.

Other combinations of functional relationships can lead to effective coping. These entail combining appropriate breathing, thoughts, feelings, and actions, as I have already listed. You should experiment with them for their functional effects with your colleagues and patient or client responsibilities. You will then be in a position to know from your own experience what combinations of relationships lead to effective coping with stress. You should find the transactional model and the categories of functional relationships are closely connected with your breathing. Notice how well you cope, and the ways the categories of functional relationships in the model are linked to your breathing. Identify those combinations which lead to effective coping and harmonious rhythmical breathing and those more inclined to increase stress and irregular breathing patterns. By practising combined coping and examining it for its effectiveness you will be able to help yourself to identify and acquire more efficient ways of dealing with stress.

THE BROADER PERSPECTIVE

Coping with stress in caring cannot be limited to the simplistic use of breathing exercises alone or one or two stress management procedures. It is as we have seen of fundamental importance to first understand stress and coping. This necessarily means appreciating the complexities of stress and coping and their relationship to different environmental demands (Bailey 1983a, 1983b; Lazarus 1981). Part of this understanding has been to consider some of the issues on stress, coping and the demands on health professionals. The specific stress control exercises can all be used to facilitate more effective coping amongst caregivers and recover, maintain and enhance their own health. I would hope this would be the least of the achievements in applying our understanding of stress and coping to good practical effect.

The broader perspective, however, means integrating all of the main aspects of stress and coping into one workable, helpful and practicable framework. How is this to be done? There is no simple answer to this question. We have seen how complex coping can be. This was pointed out clearly in the diverse range of functional relationships which can enhance or inhibit effective coping. Another way forward is to first acknowledge that we need to research and clinically evaluate how we cope with professional demands and are all of the time utilizing our perceptions of situations, breathing, thinking, feeling, and carrying out actions which influence our own functioning and quality of health care we provide. Already, there are signs that we are beginning to pay more attention to these matters (Allen 1980). Conferences in the UK, Europe, USA, New Zealand, Canada, and Australia all now share their concerns over the health of health care workers.

The study of stress management and the intricate relationships among demands, stress and coping are therefore an international priority. Mounting efforts need to be made to examine the models of professional competence presented to all health professionals (Allen 1980). Clearly, models which reflect dysfunctional and functional relationships among breathing, thinking, feeling and behaviour all help us to estimate the efficacy of our coping. In other words, these models are useful analogues informing us about people and the degree of success or difficulty in 'dealing' with their environments (Goodwin 1984).

The broader perspective on coping with stress and caring must also take into account the organizations within which health care providers work. Ultimately, it must be a marriage of individual professional responsibility and organizational responsiveness that will make desirable changes in the health professional's life. A life which daily involves coping with the demands of caring in one form or another. Much is now beginning to be done to provide the health professions with new opportunities for coping with stress (Bailey 1984a, 1984b). However, much more requires to be done by the organization of the health care system to care for those charged with the awesome responsibility of providing care. In a nutshell, there must be more new and radical ways of providing care for caregivers. I am persuaded the way ahead here is to set up counselling and consultation services for health professionals to help them better cope with the demands of caring.

CHAPTER SIX

CARING FOR
THE CAREGIVERS

You may have realized already that one of the first considerations in setting up health consultation services for health professionals must surely be whether it is presented as a restorative or preventative service. By restoration I mean a service whose fundamental orientation is to help you and other health professionals cope more effectively after they have experienced stress which interferes or impairs your caring effectiveness. Such a service should aim at restoring equilibrium and previous psychobiological functioning to a previously desired level or at least ameliorating present stress problems and features possibly associated with burn-out (Bailey 1981).

But as we have seen the present range of limited facilities for health professionals appears to work on the restorative principle — taking referrals from nurses and other health professionals when stress is already evident (Bailey 1983b, 1984a; Baldwin 1983; HMSO 1975). This is more likely to be amenable to intervention and counselling services. You will recall we observed earlier, however, that some health professionals may be seriously impaired and evidence a considerable range of stress problems making them professionally ineffective. Coping efforts here are likely to be maladaptive: with cost to caregivers' and their clients' coping. Establishing a health professional consultation service aimed at restoring effective coping should help many. However, consultations to prevent stress occuring are equally important and desirable.

A service aimed at avoiding undesirable stress and portrayed in preventive terms would act as a coping 'buffer' for many health professionals. In this sense you can envisage the health professional consultation service acting as a mediating coping mechanism. Its main purpose would obviously be to assist you and related health professionals to *avoid* getting to the point where different forms of stress such as anger, anxiety and despair and somatic complaints become serious problems. Another benefit you could encourage is developing its function as a resource bank of direct coping and social support from colleagues. Thus, the main fuctions of a health consultation service aimed at preventing stress would be to promote your existing health and maintain it wherever possible. Compliance with health consultation services to prevent stress also seems imperative if you and other health professionals are to improve their professional effectiveness. Some of these issues remain to be more closely investigated, and are clearly the topics for future research in the field of coping and caring. For the moment we can also be doing something about it in practical terms. In practical terms, health consultation services combining restorative and preventative facilities to aid health professionals coping are desirable. One immediate goal is for us to identify those facets of a health consultation service that should be included or excluded to facilitate effective coping amongst caregivers.

INCLUSION AND EXCLUSION

Who should be involved in the setting up and provision of health professional consultation services? This is a central question which you should consider carefully if you are interested in establishing counselling-coping facilities for health professionals. In designing and researching a health professional consultation service you should encourage government representatives, administrators, clinicians, and researchers to work together. They should identify criteria such as:

1   the location of the health professional support services
2   the resource personnel to be employed in the service
3   the range of techniques/facilities to provide training and reduce stress and promote effective coping

4   the goals of the health professional consultation service
5   the place of confidentiality in the provision of health professionals consultation services
6   the status of the health professional consultation services
within the general framework of health care provision

Another question you should find helpful to clarify is how the
organization that employs you and a broader range of health
care professionals relates to the health professionals consultation service. You will probably have to raise other issues from
time to time. For instance, a code of ethics for health professionals consultation services might have to be drawn up. Also
you will have to decide if client groups should be made aware of
health professionals who are attending health profession
support services as an aid to increasing their coping effectiveness (Bailey 1983a). Whatever your circumstances, questions of
this nature and criteria setting will necessarily mean deciding on
those features and functions which should be included and those
which are excluded from the establishment of providing care
services for the health professions.

With the increasing research and demand within the field for
health professional consultation services, it soon becomes
apparent that a model of health professional consultation
services is required. You have to make decisions about the form
of the service to be provided and who will administer it, and how
it is to be evaluated. It may be quite explicit which model is to be
adopted and how to organize, practise and research the HPCS
for its relationship to the health professional functioning. I shall
mention some of the considerations you might find useful in progressing towards the establishment of creative health professional consultation service models.

HEALTH PROFESSIONAL CONSULTATION
SERVICE (HPCS)

You should find a number of points are worth making about
health consultation models (e.g., HPCS). You should make

explicit what type of model is to operate. For instance, is it to be based on what is generally termed the *medical model* of illness, disease and cure (Illich 1977)? If you adopt a medical model for the HPCS it assumes 1) stress and coping are essentially medical problems, and 2) the medical profession should staff and administer health professional consultation services. (Bailey 1983a, 1983b; Bailey & Clarke in preparation). I regard stress and coping as essentially a psychological matter (see also Lazarus 1966, 1976, 1981 for seminal accounts of this issue). The HPCS should therefore be staffed by professions who are mainly concerned with the psychological processes of stress and coping. The staff should be nurses, psychologists, occupational therapists, and social workers. I would not recommend that any HPCS should adopt a narrowly specified medical approach to the care of other health professionals. I would prefer to see an interdisciplinary staffed model providing support services and stress management training with nurses and allied health professional groups. Second, a holistic or at least psychobiological learning approach to stress and coping should be incorporated into the HPCS. As I have tried to show in these pages, a cognitive-appraisal-environmental transactional relationship model of helping health professionals would also be desirable. You could easily organize and administer it so as to provide different methods of stress management training and collective-coping facilities for health professionals who wish to reduce present stress problems. Preventative functions of such an HPCS should be advertized and incorporated into each profession's service training. An underlying assumption of this psychologic-environmental approach to stress and coping is learning. From it health professions will be able to inform themselves of:

1   stress and burn-out amongst professional caregivers
2   how it comes about
3   the typical signs and symptoms
4   how we learn to produce stress by the appraisals we make and the coping efforts we attempt to make to overcome stress
5   how relearning can involve helpful stress management

and collective-coping options as ways of overcoming present stress problems and avoiding them in the future.

Finally, you can investigate the central proposal of the HPCS by monitoring and evaluating the value of its service to health professions.

In a word you should be able to research your own effectiveness in helping health professionals to manage, overcome, avoid, and prevent stress in themselves. Overall then, I suggest we adopt a broad-based cross-professional model of provision for helping health professionals to deal with stress and facilitate effective coping with the diverse occupational demands made upon them. Such a model would look something like Figure 9:

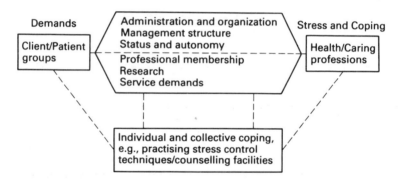

Fig. 9 Proposed model of consultation services offered to health professionals.

You can see how the model in Figure 9 can accommodate to health professionals' stress and coping, alongside the demands made from their professional commitments. Also notice how the model allows us to consider interaction with the organization of health care, and any collective coping through the provision of social support systems for health professionals. You can see an allowance is also made for the relationship between demands, stress and coping as a process over time and the kinds of adaptive or maladaptive outcomes that may be relevant to each health professional. Such a model can also be used to research and evaluate health professional functioning, the efficiency of individual and collective coping and their relationship to patient care services (Bailey 1983a, 1984c). In essence this is a psycho-educational model. You should find it a practically useful analogue of stress and coping for the health professional and it is more clinically relevant for the provision of health professional consultation service analyses than others such as the medical model (Illich 1975). This model also makes it possible to research the service it offers to health professionals and to apply the results of 'good' counselling practice (Bailey 1981) and offer coping facilities and monitor their desirability for helping the health professional to cope more effectively with stress.

Organizational Guidelines

Another major task of any HPCS is to set explicit organizational guidelines for the health professions which they employ. Typical priorities of the HPCS you might set here are:

1   Setting clear job descriptions for any personnel connected directly or indirectly with the HPCS

2   Providing a clear statement of the HPCS functions, e.g., list of services, research-evaluation, confidentiality, etc.

3   Specifying who is to be included and excluded in the execution of the HPCS functions and its responsibilities

4   Defining the roles of the HPCS and its variously associated resource support personnel

5   Constructing the model of the HPCS to be operational in the service of health professionals

You should find all these priorities and others such as the place of the HPCS in the organizational structure and its relationship to the administration have to be ironed out *before* embarking on the hasty but shaky founding of health professional consultation services. By not taking these issues into consideration and gaining support from organization managers and administrators you run the risk of making it more difficult to provide a deeply

desired but largely ignored service for nurses and their colleagues in associated health professions (Bailey 1981, 1982a,
1982b; Jones 1978). When a valid exercise takes these organizational guidelines into account you should also find it more
effective to produce documents outlining the kind of HPCS you
want and the way in which it can be managed. It follows from all
we have said that an HPCS profile would seem to be a prere-
quisite condition for the development and establishment of
health professional consultation services. By taking the time to
consider, discuss, plan, and draw up organizational guidelines,
it means that the HPCS can be inspected at any given time in its
life. This need not belie any confidentiality. What you should be
able to do is associate the HPCS with the over-all strategy of
health care and its responsibility to those to whom it offers a
service. Another benefit is you can promote and make caregivers more aware, in general terms, of the facilities available to
caregivers through the HPCS. All these issues should be the
focus of our critical consideration for they all bear on the *status*
of the HPCS and its standing within the over-all scheme of health
services provision.

Status of the HPCS

The status of any health professional consultation service should
not be overlooked in the planning stages or public image of such a
service. This issue should be of central concern to any organizational efforts you are involved with to help health professionals such as nurses function more effectively. A primary
consideration for instance is the professional autonomy of the
HPCS. This should be explicitly acknowledged by organizations
such as hospitals and documented in their various publications
about HPCS facilities (Baldwin 1983). Insufficient attention to
the status of the HPCS is likely to leave you with too many ambi-
guous aspects of a service which can only lead to misunder-
standing and conflicts of interest. There are no comprehensive
HPCS facilities in the UK or Australia, Canada and New Zealand
on the scale I have described here. If you are connected with

the planning of HPCS facilities and those who run them you may well wish to establish the standing of the service before charging full flight into setting up health professional support systems. Stanford University Hospital Nurse Consultation Service is held in considerably high esteem not only by nurses but also by care-givers in general, the University and hospital management and nurse administration (Baldwin 1983). I confirmed this for myself at Stanford in 1983. I found five characteristics which you may find helpful to enhance the status of a nurse consultation service. These are probably also applicable to HPCS facilities in general.

Characteristics of a High Status HPCS

THE HEALTH PROFESSIONALS

The relevance and importance of HPCS should be publicized and its importance for health professional functioning-effectiveness (e.g., in newsletters, memoranda, seminars, workshops, booklets and benefit lists such as learning more problem-solving skills, i.e., conflict resolution and developing more effective coping).

MANAGEMENT AND ADMINISTRATION

The general benefits of providing an HPCS should be regularly and frequently made known to management and administrations (e.g., savings to be made from less sickness absence, higher morale and job satisfaction, etc.) Though of course you should aim to preserve confidentiality. You can do this by commu-nicating only the trends rather than the identities of the individuals.

IMAGE OF CARE

The image of care you present to health professionals ought to be widened to reflect a philosophy of 'Caring for caregivers'. This image should be backed up by actual practice and the delivery of individual and collective coping opportunities for health professionals. You can increase appreciation of the caring for caregivers image. One way of doing this is by encouraging communications to the public. For instance you can do this through personal contact, contact with schools, professional training and through radio and television publicity. In other words you can help socialize the public into a broader accept-ance of health care which entails caring for health professionals themselves and helping them to develop more effective coping to deal with the demands of caring (Bailey 1983b). This is a vital challenge for the future development of consultation services for the health professions.

ECONOMIES AND SETTINGS

A further central characteristic of the HPCS should also be the economies it offers you and the settings within which it provides a service to health professionals such as nurses etc. You should make it clear what 'psychological savings' can be made in pro-moting health professionals' health and their effectiveness to cope with the demands of caring. For instance, economies may be made for the management of the service to patients. You should find this appeals to cost-conscious administrators who are concerned with getting value for money out of the health service. A high status HPCS should therefore take economic and management factors into close consideration as they are bound to play an important role in the planning and evaluation of con-sultation services for health professionals. In tandem with economic and management issues, the HPCS can show how valu-able it is in general, and in particular for the wide range of health service settings which it serves.

PROFESSIONAL AUTONOMY

The status of each HPCS is likely to be reflected in the amount of professional autonomy it has within organizations such as the hospital and general health service facilities. One indication of high professional autonomy you should aim for is for the HPCS to keep entirely confidential the results of their consultations with those health professionals which seek their help. Another you might consider is the need for hospital health authorities in particular, and health services management in general, to emphatically give their full backing to the HPCS, its aims, functions and policies.

INDIVIDUAL AND COLLECTIVE COPING

With these clear organizational guidelines, professional autonomy and an explicit model of an HPCS, it should also make it easier for you to evaluate individual and collective coping. This is an important role for any consultation service intended to help the helping professions. In striving to evaluate individual and collective coping by health professionals, you will be in a position to discover those coping tactics and coping strategies which have adaptive and maladaptive outcomes. You will find these in turn can be assessed for their short-term and long-term influence as coping alternatives for the health professionals' own health.

You should also be in a better position to identify those coping efforts by nurses and allied health professionals such as doctors, social workers and paramedical therapists, which mitigate against the efficient delivery of patient care services. Undoubtedly, a key function of any HPCS will be to monitor and evaluate and analyse the efficiency of the service that it offers to the health professions within a clearly understood HPCS model. Another is to consider the benefits and savings that might accrue to your health authority providing HPCS facilities for its employees.

RESEARCHING PRACTICE AND PRACTISING RESEARCH

To do this job effectively, and increase the efficient operation of the HPCS you should have two cardinal rules incorporated into its structure. Simply stated we should actively:

1   research the practice of the HPCS and

2   put into practice in the HPCS the results of research relevant to better understanding and facilitating more effective health professional coping.

THE PLACE OF COPING IN CARING

Clearly, we can see there is an important role for the HPCS to play in enabling nurses and allied health professionals to cope with the stress of caring. We should move forward in establishing health professional consultation services and models to meet this challenge. You can become associated with national and international developments to research and evaluate the place of coping in caring for patient and client groups and other demands relevant to the provision of health professional services. The main benefits here lie in the promise of more optimal coping being developed to aid the physical and psychological and emotional health of the health professions. You can also emphasize additional attractions such as the savings to be made by the administration and management responsible for running a caring and efficient range of health services.

Particular attention should also be extended to consider the short-term and longer-term effects of coping on health professional functioning and patient services. I believe four main areas can be identified:

1   Coping that is enhancing to professional and patient functioning

2   Coping that is enhancing to professional functioning but detrimental to patients and patient groups

3   Coping that is enhancing to patient functioning but mitigates against health professional health-effectiveness

4   Coping which is damaging to both health professional and patient-client group functioning

You should find that coping possibilities and their relationships to health professional functioning and patient care is a fundamental task for the future. Any HPCS cannot ignore the seriousness of stress amongst nurses and those in allied health professions such as medicine, social work, occupational therapy, physiotherapy, and teaching. Neither can we avoid the conclusion that caring for others can damage our own health (Bailey 1983a). As we have previously observed, sometimes our attempts to cope with the stress generated by the demands of caring can even increase various forms of stress amongst nurses and doctors and related professions. Sceptics may say providing services to help caregivers cope with caring only adds to the stress problems already encountered by health professionals. I don't accept this view. But it is salutory to note that stress is more likely to occur in those health professionals whose daily endeavours are to help patient and client groups in their care. We must express more openly that coping with caring can lead to circumstances which are often detrimental to our own health, of the caring professional and sometimes patients in our own care. I have called these circumstances the paradoxes of coping with caring (Bailey 1983a). These paradoxes can often add to the demands of caring and lead to unbelievable stress in the health care professions. These demands require the mobilization of competent coping from nurses and other health professionals. At present we have paid insufficient attention to helping health professionals overcome some of the demands made on them that lead to stress and burn-out. A start can and has to be made though. I would suggest we can do this by:

1 identifying those demands with which individuals and groups of health professionals do cope effectively
2 acknowledging the kinds of disabling and undesirable stress amongst health professions
3 showing the health professions we appreciate these stress-related problems
4 helping health professions to better understand professional stress demands and coping by the use of a practical stress and coping model and stress-coping profiles
5 showing health professionals a range of practical coping alternatives for managing stress

6   seeing the need and justification to plan, develop and establish health professional consultation services (HPCS) to enhance individual and collective coping.

The research and views I have expressed all point to the need to help develop and support health professionals cope more effectively with stress and the demands of caring. Some efforts are already being made in this direction. A move from informal and unsystemative support systems, for instance, is taking place towards more formal and systematic counselling and consultation services for nurses (Bailey 1981, 1982a; Jones 1978; Baldwin 1983). I would like to see similar models adopted for the health professionals in general and researched and evaluated for their influence in facilitating adaptive, individual and collective coping (Bailey 1983a, 1983b; 1984c). A number of issues have to be addressed. The most important is setting up health professional consultation services for caregivers.

However, a great deal remains to be done before we can regard the shift in emphasis towards 'Caring for caregivers' as part of a typical health service facility. Some, or all, of the ideas I have described in this book may be adopted. You may initiate and innovate others more appropriate and relevant to caring for caregivers. However these may be created and introduced, they must be researched and practised as part of a comprehensive consultation service for health professionals. When these changes take place we will all have taken a practical and historically more significant leap forward towards coping with stress in caring.

APPENDICES

STRESS-CHECK SCHEDULES

Practical stress-check schedules can be used along with the stress-control techniques. The use of the schedules outlined here is not compulsory for the health professional, but they are very helpful practical guidelines to be carried out in combination with stress-control training and evaluating their effectiveness for individuals and groups. They are based on a 'before' and 'after' practice principle. They involve taking baseline measures and evaluations after stress-control training interventions.

APPENDIX 1

GENERAL RELAXATION

Schedule one is of the general relaxation — 'intense stress' — calm kind. I have found it of practical benefit working with health professionals who want to reduce their general stress level. In particular, it helps practitioners to focus on the degree of stress they experience before and after a stress-control training period. It can be used in conjunction with any of the stress-control training procedures.

Before doing your stress control, you will find it helpful to set up a relaxation record similar to the example on the facing page. You would record the date and time and circle the number which shows how you feel. Then, after your stress control period, you would circle the number which indicates how relaxed you then feel.

Practise stress control and keep a relaxation record for 2 weeks; then describe how you feel generally now.

RELAXATION RECORD

		BEFORE	AFTER
DATE	TIME	Very Calm Very Tense	Very Calm Very Tense
Sun.	00:00	0 1 2 3 4 5 6 7 8 9	0 1 2 3 4 5 6 7 8 9
Mon.	00:00	0 1 2 3 4 5 6 7 8 9	0 1 2 3 4 5 6 7 8 9
Tues.	00:00	0 1 2 3 4 5 6 7 8 9	0 1 2 3 4 5 6 7 8 9
Wed.	00:00	0 1 2 3 4 5 6 7 8 9	0 1 2 3 4 5 6 7 8 9
Thurs.	00:00	0 1 2 3 4 5 6 7 8 9	0 1 2 3 4 5 6 7 8 9
Fri.	00:00	0 1 2 3 4 5 6 7 8 9	0 1 2 3 4 5 6 7 8 9
Sat.	00:00	0 1 2 3 4 5 6 7 8 9	0 1 2 3 4 5 6 7 8 9
Sun.	00:00	0 1 2 3 4 5 6 7 8 9	0 1 2 3 4 5 6 7 8 9
Mon.	00:00	0 1 2 3 4 5 6 7 8 9	0 1 2 3 4 5 6 7 8 9
Tues.	00:00	0 1 2 3 4 5 6 7 8 9	0 1 2 3 4 5 6 7 8 9
Wed.	00:00	0 1 2 3 4 5 6 7 8 9	0 1 2 3 4 5 6 7 8 9
Thurs.	00:00	0 1 2 3 4 5 6 7 8 9	0 1 2 3 4 5 6 7 8 9
Fri.	00:00	0 1 2 3 4 5 6 7 8 9	0 1 2 3 4 5 6 7 8 9
Sat.	00:00	0 1 2 3 4 5 6 7 8 9	0 1 2 3 4 5 6 7 8 9

APPENDIX 2

STRESS AUDIT

A practical stress audit, such as the following, may be done individually or in groups, after which you may discuss the effects your stress level may be having on your own health.

1 Have you been drinking, smoking or eating more than usual? YES/NO

2 Do you have difficulty sleeping at night? YES/NO

3 Are you more 'touchy' and argumentative than normal? YES/NO

4 Do you have trouble with your boss? YES/NO

5 Have you or a loved one experienced a serious illness recently? YES/NO

6 Have you been recently divorced or separated? YES/NO

7 Has there been an increase in the number of marital or family arguments? YES/NO

8 Have you been experiencing sexual difficulties? YES/NO

9 Has a close relative or friend died recently? YES/NO

10 Have you married or recently started living with someone? YES/NO

11 Has there been a pregnancy or birth in your family? YES/NO

12 Do you have financial problems? YES/NO

13 Have you recently been dismissed from work? YES/NO

14 Do you feel jumpy and on edge, flying off the handle at little things? YES/NO

15 Do you watch television more than three hours a day? YES/NO

16 Have you recently been in trouble with the law? YES/NO
17 Has there been an increase in the number of
    deadlines or work hours you are working?   YES/NO
18 Have you moved or changed the place where
    you live in the last few months?   YES/NO
19 Do you have trouble with your in-laws?   YES/NO
20 Do you feel you are exposed to constant noise at
    home or work?   YES/NO

If you have answered 'yes' this many times:

1-5   Stress is not likely to cause you any problems.
6-10   Stress is moderate and will not harm you if you
        watch your diet and get rest.
11-15   Try to eliminate some of the stress in your life or
        you risk suffering poor health.
16-20   Stress is excessive for you and you run the risk of
        developing a major illness.

APPENDIX 3

BURN-OUT INVENTORY

Schedule three is a Burn-out Inventory which may be completed by setting up a Burn-out Checklist similar to the example on the facing page. On your checklist simply make a check against each item which applies to you. A number of stress-checks may be carried out (e.g., before, during and after practising stress control). By doing this you could compare the items you have checked on the Burn-out Checklist with the practice of stress-control training. You may wish to keep a separate note of any changes that have taken place and benefits which you have observed.

PROCEDURE

1   Draw up your own Burn-out Checklist and on it make a check mark against any item as it applies to you at present.

2   Add up the number of items you have checked, e.g., 10 burn-out items.

3   Select an appropriate stress-control technique and put it into practice.

4   Practise stress control for a specific number of weeks (e.g., 1, 4, 6, 10 etc.)

5   After completing each practice period, reassess yourself on your Burn-out Inventory.

6   Now make any comparisons with your previous assessment.

7   If you are satisfied, you may stop stress-control training. But if you want to, continue with the same stress-control training or other stress-control procedures.

8   Repeat any reassessment and further stress-control training if necessary.

Note: You may find it helpful to discuss items on your Burn-out Inventory and stress-control training programme with your colleagues, tutor-advisor or counsellor.

BURN-OUT CHECKLIST

	Assessment				
	1	2	3	4	5

1 High resistance to going to work every day.

2 A sense of failure.

3 Anger and resentment.

4 Guilt and blame.

5 Discouragement and indifference.

6 Negativism.

7 Isolation and withdrawal.

8 Feeling tired and exhausted all day.

9 Frequent clockwatching.

10 Great fatigue after work.

11 Loss of positive feelings towards clients/patients.

12 Postponing client contacts; resisting client phone calls and office visits.

13 Stereotyping clients.

14 Inability to concentrate or listen to what clients or colleagues are saying.

15 Feeling immobilized.

16 Cynicism regarding clients-colleagues; a blaming attitude.

17 Increasingly 'going by the book'.

18 Sleep disorders.

19 Avoiding discussion of work with colleagues.

20 Self-preoccupation.

21 More approving of behaviour-control measures such as tranquillizers.

22 Frequent colds and flus.

23 Frequent headaches.

24 Rigidity in thinking and resistance to change.

25 Suspicion and paranoia.

26 Excessive use of drugs e.g., alcohol, tobacco products, etc.

27 Marital and family conflict.

28 High absenteeism.

29 Skin complaints, e.g., rashes etc.

30 Gastrointestinal disturbances.

Number of symptoms

APPENDIX 4

STRESS-INNOCULATION
TRAINING (SIT)

STRESS-CONTROL SCHEDULES

1   List the situations or demands you have difficulty in coping with effectively.

2   Detail the kinds of behaviour, thoughts and feelings you have, and the forms of stress they generate.

3   Now practise stress-innoculation training (SIT) and apply the programme to the demands/situations you have listed (see pp. 103–9 for SIT programme).

4   Practise for 1, 2, 3, 4, 5, 6 or more weeks and note any differences in the situations or demands which previously led to stress. Note also any altered behaviour, thoughts, and feelings, and the change, if any, in your reported stress level.

5   Remember to compliment yourself and tell others you regard as important, and whom you respect, how well you are doing (if you are getting positive results).

6   Regularly rehearse (at least 2–3 times per day) your SIT programme in your imagination and put it into practice each day.

7   Keep a note of any success, and detail where it is taking place in your stress-control practice (e.g., less intense demands, situations still troublesome but can tolerate them better, feel less anxious, angry, depressed, frustrated, etc., I did well, someone important noticed I had control today, and so on).

8   A personal diary of these events laid out in a systematic way will be of great benefit in reviewing your practice of stress-innoculation training, and progressive steps towards more effective stress control.

APPENDIX 5

JOB APPRAISAL SCALE

Sometimes the way we appraise our job can give us a useful guide to how stressful it is for us. There is no ideal questionnaire that would suit all circumstances and work conditions. These have to be designed to evaluate specific jobs. This questionnaire, devised by the Association of Scientific and Managerial Staffs (ASTMS), shows how you may analyse whether your job offers you enough scope and satisfaction. As on page 154, you could consider the following questionnaire and make a separate note of your responses.

Do you agree with the following statements?

1 I find on the whole, my work is varied and interesting. YES/NO

2 Generally, the work load is not too heavy. YES/NO

3 I feel my job makes good use of my skills. YES/NO

4 I am satisfied with the amount of responsibility that goes with my job. YES/NO

5 I am rarely asked to make decisions above the level of my responsibility. YES/NO

6 I do not find there is too much hustle and bustle. YES/NO

7 I find I can generally complete my work in the time allowed. YES/NO

8 I have been trained adequately for the work I do. YES/NO

9 I find in spite of my training and skills I can still go on learning. YES/NO

10 For most of the time I have a clear understanding of what is expected of me in my work. YES/NO

11   Good work is recognized by my employer and
offers chances of promotion.   YES/NO

12   I understand and agree with my job description
in comparison with other grades and people in the
company think I am properly rewarded for the
work I do.   YES/NO

13   Although I may not like the outcome, at least we
have a recognized procedure to follow if I have a
complaint.   YES/NO

14   If changes in work methods or equipment are
under consideration we are always consulted.   YES/NO

15   My department is adequately staffed.   YES/NO

16   Generally, working conditions are good with
few difficulties over noise, heat or vibrations.   YES/NO

How many 'No's' did you mark?

4 or under	Possible scope for improvement but nothing is perfect.
5–10	Plenty of opportunity for improvements.
Over 10	See your class or group representative immediately, or think about changing your job.

REFERENCES

ABRAMSON L., SELIGMAN M. & TEASDALE J. (1978) Learned helplessness in humans: critique and reformulation. *Journal of Abnormal Behaviour* **87**, 49–74.

ALLEN H. (1980) *The Ward Sister*. Heinemann, London.

ALLIBONE A., OAKES D. & SHANNON H.S. (1979) Report on the Health of Doctors. A medical study funded by the East Anglian Regional Health Authority under the NHS Locally Organized Research Scheme 1977–9. TUC Centenary Institute of Occupational Health and London School of Hygiene and Tropical Medicine, London.

—— (1981) The health and health care of doctors. *Journal of the Royal College of General Practitioners* **31**, 728–34.

ANNANDALE-STEINER D. (1979a) Unhappiness is the nurse who expected more. *Nursing Mirror* November 29, 34–6.

—— (1979b) The nurse counsellor role at Guy's. *Nursing Times* August 13, 1345–9.

ANSELL E.M. (1981) Professional burn-out: recognition and management. *Journal of the American Association of Nurse Anaesthetists* **49**, 135–42.

ARNDT C. & LAEGER E. (1970a) Role strain in a diversified role set: the Director of Nursing Service. Part 1. *Nursing Research* **19**, 253–9.

—— (1970b) Role strain in a diversified role set: the Director of Nursing Service. Part II. *Sources of Stress Nursing Research* **19**, 495–501.

BAILEY R. (1980) Stress and Nurses. Unpublished seminar, High Wycombe School of Nursing.

—— (1981) Counselling services for nurses — a forgotten responsibility. *Journal British Institute of Mental Handicap* **9**, 45–7.

—— (1982a) Counselling services for nurses. *Journal of the British Association for Counselling*, B.A.C. Publications **39**, 25–39.

—— (1982b) Burn-out, Human Social Functioning and the Helping Professions 1–12. Proceedings of 1st British Conference on Human Social Functioning. Chelmsford, Essex, England.

—— (1983a) Stress and Coping with the Demands of Caring. Seminar, School of Nursing and School of Medicine, University of California, San Francisco.

161

—— (1983b) The ART and Science of Kicking the Sickness Habit. Seminar, School of Nursing and School of Medicine, University of California, San Francisco.

—— (1984a) Autogenic Regulation Training and sickness absence amongst nurses in general training. *Journal of Advanced Nursing* **9**, 581–8.

—— (1984b) Stop Seething and Start Breathing. Journal Club Address, Manor House Hospital, Aylesbury, Bucks, England.

—— (1984c) Opportunities for Coping with Stress. Kings Fund Centre, London.

BAILEY R. & CLARKE M. (in prep.) *Stress and Coping in Nursing*. Croom Helm, London.

BAILEY R., BAILEY J. & CHIRIBOGA D. (1983) Conceptual Methodological and Research Issues in the Study of Stress. Doctoral seminars, School of Nursing and School of Medicine University of San Francisco.

BAILEY R., CHIRIBOGA D. & LARSON K. (1983). Personal communication. Postdoctoral seminar, School of Nursing, University of San Francisco.

BAKAL D. (1979) *Psychology and Medicine*. Tavistock, London.

BALDWIN A. (1983) How Nurses Cope Successfully with Stress: A Stanford Nursing Department Study. Stanford University Hospital, California, 1–9.

BANDURA A. (1977) Self-efficacy: toward a unifying theory of behavioural change. *Psychology Review* **84**, 191–215.

BARTON D. (1977a) Dying, death and bereavement as health care problems. In Barton D. (ed.) *Dying and Death. A Clinical Guide for Caregivers*, ch 1. Williams and Wilkins, Baltimore.

—— (1977b) The Caregiver. In Barton D. (ed.) *Dying and Death. A Clinical Guide for Caregivers*, ch 6. Williams and Wilkins, Baltimore.

BECK A. (1972) *Depression: Causes and Treatment*. International University Press, New York.

—— (1976) *Cognitive Therapy and The Emotional Disorders*. International University Press, New York.

BENNET G. (1982) Sick doctors — ourselves. *Update* **24**, 1621–31. The Journal of Postgraduate Medical Practice.

BENSON H. (1980) *The Relaxation Response*. Fount Paperbacks, Collins, Glasgow.

—— ROSNER B.A., MARZETTA B.R. & KLEMCHUK H.M. (1974) Decreased blood pressure in borderline hypertensive subjects who practised meditation. *Journal of Chronic Diseases* **27**, 163–9.

BIRCH J. (1979) The anxious learners. *Nursing Mirror* February 8, 17–24.

BIRX E. (1983) Identifying Stressors and Satisfiers of Neonatal Intensive Care Nurses. MSc thesis, School of Nursing, University of Rochester, New York.

BLACHLY P.H., DISHER W. & RODUNER G. (1968) Suicide by physicians. *Bulletin of Suicidology* **1**, 1–18.

BLOOMFIELD H.H., CAIN M.P., JAFFE D.T. & KORY R.B. (1975) *TM — Discovering Inner Energy and Overcoming Stress.* Dell, New York.

BRITISH MEDICAL JOURNAL (1979) Alcohol-dependent doctors. Editorial. *B.M.J.* **2**, 351.

CANNON W.B. (1932) *The Wisdom of the Body.* Norton, New York.

CAPLAN G. & KILLILEA M. (eds) (1976) *Support Systems and Mutual Help.* Grune and Stratton, New York.

CHARLESWORTH E.A., MURPHY S. & BEUTLER L.E. (1981) Stress management for nursing students. *Journal of Clinical Psychology* **37**, 284–90.

CHERNISS C. (1980) *Staff Burnout: Job Stress in the Human Services.* Sage, London.

CHIRIBOGA, D. (1983) Personal communication.

CLAUS K. & BAILEY J. (eds) (1980) *Living with Stress and Promoting Well-Being.* C.V. Mosby, St. Louis.

COLLIGAN M., SMITH M. & HORREL J. (1977) Occupational incidence rates of mental health disorders. *Journal of Human Stress* **3**, 34–42.

CRAMMER J.L. (1978) Psychosis in young doctors. *B.M.J.* **1**, 560–1.

EDELWICH J. & BRODSKY A. (1980) *Burn-out: Stages of Disillusionment in the Helping Professions.* The Human Science Press, New York.

FINE C. (1981) *Married to Medicine: an Intimate Portrait of 'Doctors' Wives.* Atheneum, New York.

FOLKMAN S. (1983) If it changes it must be a process: a study of emotions and coping during three stages of a college examination. *Journal of Personality and Social Psychology* (in press).

—— & LAZARUS, R. (1980) An analysis of coping in a middle-aged community sample. *Journal of Health and Social Behaviour* **21**, 219–39.

FREUDENBERGER H.J. (1974) Staff burn-out. *Journal of Social Issues* **30**, 159–65.

FREUDENBERGER H.J. (1975) The staff burn-out syndrome in alternative institutions. *Psychotherapy: Theory, Research and Practice* **12**, 73–82.

GARBER J. & SELIGMAN M. (eds) (1980) *Human helplessness: theory and applications.* Academic, New York.

GARDAM J.F. (1969) Nursing stresses in the intensive care unit (letters to the editor). *Journal of American Medical Association (JAMA).*

GLASER B.G. & STRAUSS A.L. (1965) *Awareness of Dying.* Aldine, Chicago.
—— (1968) *Time for Dying.* Aldine, Chicago.
GLASS D.C. & SINGER J.E. (1972) *Urban Stress: Experiments on Noise and Social Stressors.* Academic, New York.
GLASSER W.J. (1979) *Positive Addiction.* Harper & Row, New York.
GOLEMAN D. (1976) Meditation helps break the stress spiral. *Psychology Today* **9**, 82–6.
GOODWIN S. (1984) Personal communication. Kings Fund Conference on Stress in Nursing, London.
GUNTHER M.S. (1977) The threatened staff: a psychoanalytic contribution to medical psychology. *Comprehensive Psychiatry* **18**, 385–96.
HAY D. & OKEN D. (1972) The psychological stresses of intensive care unit nursing. *Psychosomatic Medicine* **34**, 109–18.
HESS W.R. (1957) *The Functional Organisation of the Diencephalon.* Grune and Stratton, New York.
HMSO (1972) Report of the Committee on Nursing. Chairman Professor Asa Briggs. Cmnd. No. 5115. London.
HMSO (1975) Report of the Committee of Inquiry into the Regulation of the Medical Profession. Merrison A.W.
HMSO (1978) Registrar General Decennial Supplement England and Wales. Occupational Mortality.
HOOPER J. (1979) An Exploratory Study of Student and Pupil Nurses' Attitudes Towards, and Expectation of, Nursing Geriatric Patients in Hospital. Unpublished MSc thesis, University of Surrey.
HOUSE J.S. (1981) *Work Stress and Social Support.* Addison-Wesley, Reading, Massachusetts.
HUCKABAY L.M.D. & JAGLA B. (1979) Nurses' stress factors in the intensive care unit. *Journal of Nursing Administration* **9**, 21–6.
HUGILL J. (1975) Nurse counselling. *Nursing Mirror* April 10, 58–61.
ILLICH I. (1975) *Medical Nemesis.* Calder and Boyars, London.
IRVINE D. (1982) Reported by Mary Bishop in *Family Practitioner* **12**, no. 46.
JACOBSON E. (1929) *Progressive Relaxation.* The University of Chicago Press, Chicago.
—— (1934) *You Must Relax.* Whittlesey House, New York.
JOHNSTON W. (1983) *The Mirror Mind.* Fount paperbacks, Collins, Oxford.
JONES D. (1978) The need for a comprehensive counselling service for nursing students. *Journal of Advanced Nursing* **3**, 359–68.
KAPLAN B.H., CASSEL J.C. & GORE S. (1977) Social support and health. *Medical Care* **15**, 47–58.

KRAMER M. (1974) *Reality Shock: Why Nurses Leave Nursing*. C.V. Mosby, St. Louis.

KRUMBOLTZ J.D. & THORESON C.E. (1976) (eds) *Counselling Methods*. Holt Rhinehart and Winston, New York.

KÜBLER-ROSS E. (1973) *On Death and Dying*. Social Sciences Paperbacks, London.

LAMERTON R. (1973) *Care of the Dying*. Priory, London.

—— (1978) The care of the dying: a speciality. *Nursing Times* March 16, 436.

LAVANDERO R. (1981) Nurse burn-out: what can we learn? *Journal of Nursing Administration* **11**, 17–23.

LAZARUS A. (1972) *Behaviour Therapy and Beyond*. McGraw-Hill, New York.

—— (1976) *Multi-modal Behavior Therapy*. Springer, New York.

LAZARUS, R. (1966) *Psychological Stress and the Coping Process*. McGraw-Hill, New York.

—— (1976) *Patterns of Adjustment*. McGraw-Hill, New York.

—— (1981) The stress and coping paradigm. In C. Eisdorfer, D. Cohen, A. Kleinman & P. Maxim (eds) *Models for Clinical Psychopathology*. Spectrum, New York.

—— (1983a) The costs and benefits of denial. In S. Breznitz (ed.) *The Denial of Stress*. International Universities Press, New York.

—— (1983b) The trivialization of distress. In J.C. Rosen & L.J. Solomon (eds) *Preventing Health Risk Behaviors and Promoting Coping with Illness*. Vol. 8.

LAZARUS R. & LAUNIER R. (1978) Stress-related transactions between person and environment. In L.A. Dervin & M. Lewis (eds) *Perspectives in International Psychology*. Plenum, New York.

LEE P.N. (1979) Has the mortality of male doctors improved with the reductions in their cigarette smoking? *B.M.J.* **2**, 1538–40.

LEFCOURT H. (1976) *Locus of Control: Current Trends in Theory and Research*. Wiley, New York.

LINDEMANN H. (1974) *Relieve Tension the Autogenic Way*. Abelard-Schuman, London.

LLOYD G. (1982) I am an alcoholic. *B.M.J.* 285, 785–6.

LUTHE W. (1963) Autogenic state and autogenic shift. *Acta Psychotherapeutica et Psychosomatica* **11**, 1–13.

—— & BLUMBERGER, S.R. (1977) Autogenic therapy. In Eric D. Wittkower & Hector Warnes (eds) *Psychosomatic Medicine: Its Clinical Applications*. Harper & Row, London.

McCONNELL E. (1982) *Burnout in the Nursing Profession*. C.V. Mosby, St. Louis.

McCUE J.D. (1980) The effects of stress on physicians and their medical practice. *New England Journal of Medicine* **306**, 456–63.

—— (1982) *Private Practice: Surviving the First Year*. Collemore Lexington, Massachusetts.

MARSHALL J. (1980) Stress amongst nurses. In C. Cooper & J. Marshall (eds) *White Collar and Professional Stress*. Wiley, London.

MASLACH C. (1976) Burned-out. *Human Behaviour* **5**, 16–22.

—— & PINES, A. (1977) The burn-out syndrome in the day care setting. *Child Care Quarterly* **6**, 100–13.

MEICHENBAUM D. (1979) *Cognitive-Behaviour Modification*. Plenum, New York.

MENZIES I. (1960) Institutional defence against anxiety. *Human Relations* **13**, 95–121.

MICHAELS D. (1971) Too much in need of support to give any? *American Journal of Nursing* **71**, 1932–5.

MOORE J. (1984) Helping nurses cope. *Nursing Times*. October 17, 47–8.

MOORES B. & GRANT G.W.B. (1977) Feelings of alienation among nursing staff in hospitals for the mentally handicapped. *International Journal of Nursing Studies* **14**, 5–12.

MOOS R. (1979) *Coping with Physical Illness*. Plenum, New York.

MURRAY R.M. (1976) Alcoholism amongst male doctors in Scotland. *The Lancet* **2**, 729–31.

MURRAY R.M. (1978) The health of doctors: a review. *Journal of The Royal College of Physicians of London* **12**, 403–15.

—— (1983) The Mentally ill doctor: causes and consequences. *The Practitioner* **222**, 65–75.

MURRAY PARKES C. (1970) The psychosomatic effects of bereavement. In Oscar W. Hill (ed.) *Modern Trends in Psychosomatic Medicine*, vol 2. Butterworths, London.

—— (1978) Psychological aspects. In C.M. Saunders (ed.) *The Management of Terminal Diseases*. Edward Arnold, London.

—— (1980) *Bereavement: Studies of Grief in Adult Life*. Pelican, London.

NEISSER U. (1972) *Cognitive Psychology*. McGraw-Hill, New York.

NURSE G. (1975) *Counselling and the Nurse*. HM & M, Aylesbury.

OSWIN M. (1971) *The Empty Hours*. Allen Lane, London.

—— (1978) *Children Living in Long-stay Hospital*. Spastics International, Lavenham Press, Suffolk.

PARKES, K. (1980a) Occupational stress among nurses — 1. A comparison of medical and surgical wards. Occasional Papers. *Nursing Times* October 30, 113–16.

—— (1980b) Occupational stress amongst nurses — 2. A comparison of male and female wards. Occasional Papers. *Nursing Times* November 6, 117–19.

PERVIN L. (1963) The need to predict and control under conditions of threat. *Journal of Personality* **31**, 570–87.

PETERSEN W.P. (1979) *Meditation Made Easy.* Franklin Watts, New York.

RACHMAN S. (1980) Emotional processing. *Behaviour Research and Therapy* **18**, 51–60.

RAMACHAKARA Y. (1974) *Science of Breath: The Oriental Breathing Philosophy.* L.N. Fowler, London.

RARDIN M. (1969) Treatment of a phobia by partial self-desensitization. *Journal of Consulting and Clinical Psychology* **33**, 125–6.

REDFERN S. (1979) Stress in Charge Nurses. Unpublished MSc thesis, University of Manchester.

ROSA K. (1976) *Autogenic Training.* Victor Gollancz, London.

ROSE K.D. & ROSOW N.I. (1973) Physicians who kill themselves. *Archives General Psychiatry* **29**, 800–5.

ROTTER J. (1966) Generalised expectancies for internal versus external control of reinforcement. *Psychological Monographs* **80** No. 609.

ROTTER J., CHANCE J.E. & PHARES E.J. (1972) *Applications of a Social Learning Theory of Personality.* Holt, Rhinehart and Winston, New York.

SAKINOFSKY I. (1980) Suicide in doctors and their wives. Correspondence column, *B.M.J.* **281**, 386–7.

SCHULTZ J. & LUTHE W. (1959) *Autogenic Training. A Psychophysiologic Approach to Psychotherapy.* Grune and Stratton, New York.

—— (1969) *Autogenic Therapy. Autogenic Methods.* Grune and Stratton, New York.

SCHWARTZ J. (1978) *Voluntary Controls.* E.P. Dutton, New York.

SELIGMAN M. (1975) *Helplessness.* W.H. Freeman and Co., San Francisco.

SELYE H. (1980) Stress and a holistic view of health for the nursing profession. In K. Claus & J. Bailey (eds) *Living with Stress and Promoting Well-being.* C.V. Mosby, St. Louis.

SOBOL E. (1979) Self-actualization and the baccalaureate students response to stress. *Journal of Nursing Research* **27**, 238–44.

SPEILBERGER C. (1972) *Anxiety: Current Trends in Theory and Research. Vol. II.* Academic, New York.

STEFFEN S. (1980) Perception of stress: 1800 nurses tell their stories. In K. Claus & J. Bailey (eds) *Living with Stress and Promoting Well-being.* C.V. Mosby, St. Louis.

STONE G., COHEN F. & ADLER N. (1980) *Health Psychology: A Handbook.* Jossey Bass, San Francisco.

SUZUKI D.T. (1982) *Living by Zen.* Rider, London.

VAILLANT G.E., BRIGHTON J.R. & McARTHUR C. (1970) Physicians'
    use of mood-altering drugs: a twenty-year follow-up report. *New
    England Journal of Medicine* **282**, 365–70.
VAILLANT G.E., SOBOWALE N.C. & McARTHUR C. (1972) Some
    psychologic vulnerabilities of physicians. *New England Journal of
    Medicine* **287**, 372–4.
VOLIN M. (1980) *The Quiet Hour.* Pelham, London.
VREELAND R. & ELLIS G. (1969) Stresses on the nurse in an intensive
    care unit. *JAMA* **208**, 2337–8.
VON LYSEBETH A. (1983) *Pranayama: The Yoga of Breathing.* Unwin,
    Boston.
WATTS A. (1982) *The Way of Zen.* Pelican, London.
—— (1983) *The Wisdom of Insecurity.* Rider, London.
WELLENKEMP D. (1983) Personal communication. Administrator.
    Santa Barbara Cottage Hospital, California.
WHITFIELD S. (1979) A Descriptive Study of Student Nurses' Ward
    Experiences with Dying Patients and Their Attitudes Towards
    Them. Unpublished MSc thesis, University of Manchester.
WITTKOWER E.D. & WARNES H. (eds) (1977) *Psychosomatic Medicine:
    Its Clinical Applications.* Harper & Row, New York.
WOLPE J. (1958) *Psychotherapy by Reciprocal Inhibition.* Stanford
    University Press, Stanford.
—— (1973) *The Practice of Behavior Therapy.* Pergamon, New York.
—— & LAZARUS, A. (1966) *Behavior Therapy Techniques.* Pergamon,
    Oxford.
WOOD E. (1969) *Yoga.* Penguin, London.
ZASTROW C. (1979) *Talk to Yourself: Using the Power of Self-talk.*
    Spectrum, New York.

INDEX